THE SIMPLE SURVIVAL SMART BOOK

BY PATRICK J SHRIER
SFC, USA (RET)

THE SIMPLE SURVIVAL SMART BOOK

Battles & Book Reviews Publishing

ISBN-10: 0615880266
ISBN-13: 978-0615880266

For my wife Petra

With you, anything is possible, without you, nothing is.

And my son Dominik

Those conversations about what we would do during a zombie apocalypse have helped me clarify my thinking about several things.

"To live, a man needs food, water, and a sharp mind."

USAAC 2LT Louis Zamperini (US Olympian and World War II Japanese POW)

TABLE OF CONTENTS

Introduction	xii
Chapter 1 – Survival Planning	1
Chapter 2 – Preparedness Kits	11
Chapter 3 – Outdoor Survival	25
Chapter 4 – Map Reading & Navigation	53
Chapter 5 – Acquiring Food & Water	81
Chapter 6 – Combat	109
Chapter 7 – Basic Field First Aid	161
Chapter 8 – Useful and Helpful Knots	211
Appendix A – Tips, Tricks, and Hints	223
Appendix B – Minefield Record Card	225
Appendix C – Foodborne Illnesses	229
Reference List	235
Glossary	239

ABOUT THE AUTHOR

First, about me. I was a soldier, specifically a Cavalry Scout in the United States Army, for 23 years from 1989 to 2011. During that time I deployed twice, to Bosnia as part of the NATO IFOR mission from January to December 1996 and to Iraq for OIF II from February 2004 to March 2005. I spent the greater part of my career in Divisional Heavy Cavalry Squadrons with a two year tour as a Drill Sergeant, three years testing close-combat weapons & sensors, and three horrible years on staff as an Operations Senior NCO.

During my time in the US Army and during the times I was not in a line unit I managed to complete a Bachelors and Masters Degrees in History; both with Honors. My area of historical specialty, every historian has one, is Prussian history from Frederick the Great to the end of World War I. I wrote my MA thesis on the Battle of Königgrätz, the decisive battle of the Austro-Prussian War of 1866. I have been a lifelong hunter and camper and during my military career spent too many days in the field to count

More about me and my other writing can be found at my website: Battles & Book Reviews (http://www.military-history.us/). I can be contacted via email at patrick@military-history.us

INTRODUCTION

*"Liberals, it has been said, are generous with other peoples'
money, except when it comes to questions of national survival
when they prefer to be generous with other people's freedom
and security."*

**William F. Buckley, Jr. (Conservative American
Columnist)**

The reason for me to write this book were my observations on the state of society in both the United States and the rest of the world. Combining those observations with my knowledge of history, I am convinced that another civilizational interregnum similar to what occurred after the Fall of Rome will overtake Western society sooner rather than later. If you want to know why I think that read the 2nd Century Satires of _Juvenal_ (http://www.fordham.edu/halsall/ancient/juv-sat1eng.asp) and tell me he could not be writing today. In the interests of being prepared for the coming collapse and sharing the knowledge and experience from my military career and interests, I wrote this book.

My basic organizing principle in putting this volume together was to make it similar to the checklists I used during my 23 military career.

In my M3A2 Bradley Fighting Vehicle in Iraq and Bosnia I had three books that I always kept in my turret and they often came in handy. Two of them were military publications and one is a book I put together myself. The two military publications were FM 21-76: Survival and my Squadron Tactical SOP (TACSOP). The one I put together myself was a collection of all the most useful Graphical Training Aids (GTA)'s that I thought I would need in everyday combat operations and some I would only need occasionally. I have used all three books as well as the SMART Books we issued to new Privates in basic training as the inspiration for putting this book together and the way in which I chose to organize it.

The old adages that "forewarned is fore-armed" and "knowledge is power" are applicable to any survival situation. What you don't know both cannot help you and certainly might kill you. The idea is not that this book will tell you how to live the rest of your life in comfort after the apocalypse, it is to equip you with enough common sense information such that a moderately prepared person can survive to get to a place of refuge or be useful enough to somebody else that they will be accepted into theirs.

The information in this book is intended to be a starting place and reference, not a final solution. Preparedness is like anything else in life, a continual process. This book is just a place to start.

In all my discussions throughout the book I will discuss options as though there are four members in your party. It is my opinion that four is the minimum party size that can survive for any length of time in the face of both scarcity and the possibility of violence and thievery that will no doubt be prevalent after the collapse of modern society.

A note on units of measurement: I generally use Feet, Inches, and Pounds throughout the book because that is the system of measurement most Americans are familiar with. I do in some sections use metric units, mainly in the land navigation section because even USGS maps are now delineated in Meters. That is for purely practical reasons as the metric system is much better suited to cartography with its neat decimal system than is the chaotic ancient system of Feet, Yards, and Miles. If I had my way the whole world would be metric, which is probably the only really good thing to come out of Europe in the past 250 years.

A note on Illustrations: Most of the Illustrations in this book come from US Army publications and are thus in the public domain. Those that are not my own work or in the Public Domain are credited if I got them from somewhere else. I am a jerk about copyright infringement from my own published work (web or otherwise) so I figure it is only right if I treat other people's work how I expect my own to be treated.

CHAPTER 1 – SURVIVAL PLANNING

"After we have thought out everything carefully in advance and have sought and found without prejudice the most plausible plan, **we must be ready to abandon it at the slightest provocation.** *Should this certainty be lacking, we must tell ourselves that nothing is accomplished in warfare without daring; that the nature of war certainly does not let us see at all times where we are going; that what is probable will always be probable though at the moment it may not seem so; and* **finally, that we cannot be readily ruined by a single error, if we have made reasonable preparations.** *"*

Karl von Clausewitz (Military Theorist & Prussian Officer)

Before any discussion of planning can commence Murphy's Law must be mentioned. Moltke the Elder is the Prussian General who apocryphally originated the saying that *"no plan survives first contact with the enemy"* although Clausewitz alludes to much the same phenomenon in his classic *On War*. It was true 150 years ago and it was true 2,000 years ago, it is equally true today, and will be so in the future. As soon as something has to happen, it probably won't. The modern conception of this truism is called Murphy's Law, which reads: ***"If something can go wrong, IT WILL!"*** Always, and I mean always, keep that bastard Murphy in mind when you are planning anything. As sure as the Sun rises in the East, the moment you don't is when he will rear his ugly head and bite you in the behind. One thing is certain, expect Murphy to have a say in everything, especially where weapons are concerned. Your weapon will jam at the worst possible time, the demo won't blow, or just as a patrol of fifty guys walks into your ambush the Claymores won't clack. It happens, the best thing to do is drive on and always have a plan B, C, D, and even E.

You can have the best **B.O.B.** set-up in the world, more ammo than you can carry, and the best training and experience but without a logical, rational, and realistic plan all your preparations will be for nothing. Absent a decent plan you will probably die in the first few days or weeks after the World Ends. As a matter of fact, the ***absolute first*** thing you should do before starting any preparation, is come up with a plan. Write your plan down, sit on it for a week, and then review, rethink, and revise it. After 2-3 iterations of that you should have a good enough plan to start working with.

A pitfall to avoid in planning is to be either too pessimistic or on the contrary, too optimistic. There is an old military truism as applies to planning that goes *"expect victory but plan for defeat"*. If you do that you can keep your plan realistic and a realistic plan is one that is much more likely to see you survive than one that is not. Many people call realists cynics, I don't subscribe to that theory. Realists

2

see the world as it is, not as they want it to be and act accordingly.

There are actually two varieties of planning you need to consider when getting ready for the world to end. Short range and long range. Short range planning is what you do for the first week to ten days after the balloon goes up and everything goes south, long range planning is everything after that as in, the rest of your life. Short range planning should be fairly specific while long range planning is more goal oriented.

Short range planning is a constantly recurring task once the balloon goes up because every evening you should think about the next day and have a plan for it. Not only does this keep your mind occupied, it is a good habit to get into because it keeps you sharp and will tend to make you more aware of your situation and thus less likely to be surprised.

If there is one thing the military is good at, it is planning. They make plans for everything. From what to eat, where to put latrines, how to drive, to how to fight battles and wage wars. Military theory applies to everything planning related. Especially applicable is the military decision making process (MDMP) as adapted to fit civilian requirements. The MDMP is the model the military uses at all levels when it is developing plans for specific operations or actions. My purpose here is not to get you to be able to write a good Five Paragraph Operations Order (OPORD), but to get you thinking about things in an analytic manner during the planning process before the balloon goes up and the time for planning is gone because you have to act or face death or worse.

If you read the steps and then think about them for a minute you will realize that they are nothing more than an explicit rendering of the subconscious steps you automatically follow every day with just about every decision you make no matter how large or small.

There are seven steps to the MDMP and I have slightly modified them to fit the prepper's or just plain smart

The Steps of the Decision Making Process

1. Determine the objective (What is the Problem)
2. Analyze the objective (What do I want to do)
3. Develop courses of action (What can I do)
4. Analyze courses of action (What happens if I do)
5. Compare courses of action (What is best to do)
6. Determine a course of action (This is What I will do)
7. Implement course of action (Do it)

person's needs.

I will discuss each step in depth below. The importance of planning is to give you a realistic appraisal, with the emphasis on **realistic**, of the difficulty of a task and figure out how to accomplish it in the most efficient manner possible and at the least danger to yourself or your party. Keep in mind that most efficient does not necessarily mean least labor or effort intensive method.

DETERMINE THE OBJECTIVE

The Omenica River in British Columbia, Canada in 1913

The first thing you have to do is decide what your objective is going to be. In simpler terms, what are you trying to do. This can be anything from broad (be prepared) to specific (how do I cross this river). The nature of your objective will determine the way forward as you work your way through the process. I will choose a specific objective - *How do I cross this river by sundown?* You are moving from left to right in the photo? (Below)

Given the above objective as a theoretical starting point I will discuss each step and then work my way through it to illustrate how this process works, or should work if applied correctly.

ANALYZE THE OBJECTIVE

To analyze the objective means looking at it and determining what its characteristic are and what we have to overcome or work around to achieve the objective. The important part of analyzing the objective is to be realistic and not ignore the hard or difficult aspects in favor of the aspects that seem easy. It is the difficult parts that make rigorous analysis so important. Given our theoretical objective, here is the analysis I would come up with *(I have arbitrarily come up with values you cannot deduce from the picture because I have never actually been there).*

- The river is approximately 30-40 feet wide
- The approach to the river is a boulder field with a straight drop of 5-15 feet into the water depending on approach path.
- The exit from the river is a fairly steep scree slope, which means uncertain footing.
- The date on the photo indicates we are trying to cross in October. The water is therefore going to be very cold.
- The river is between 6-9 foot deep
- The water is fairly swift at 5-10 mph.
- It is mid-morning
- There are some clouds in the sky but it is generally sunny.
- You have had contact with potential hostiles within the past two days

These are the facts I have gathered based on the analysis of the situation.

Generally all an analysis consists of is a list of things you know. You can **only** plan based on what you know. Any plan based on guesses is bound to fail and doesn't merit being a called a plan at all. Once you have analyzed the situation and figured out all that you can know you have all the information you are going to get to move on to the next step.

DEVELOP COURSES OF ACTION

The third step is what I think of as the brain-storming step. This is where you let your imagination run wild and come up with scenarios that will let you achieve your objective. Don't stop yourself from thinking unconventionally, often it is unconventional thinking that leads to innovative solutions. A limitation to keep in mind during this step is your available resources in both time and material. I am assuming that all four members of your party have fully stocked B.O.B. Bags minus some food.

Many a time while planning a soldier would pipe up with something that sounded stupid at first but the more we thought about it the more workable it sounded. Crazy does not equate to undesirable in the world of planning. Below are the COA's I came up with.

a. Walk up/downstream to find a ford
b. Swim across towing a line for the rest of the party
c. Use a log/raft to float across
d. Build a boat
e. Try and jump across boulder to boulder
f. Throw a rope from one bank to the other

ANALYZE COURSES OF ACTION

This is the step where you look at each COA and determine the resources you need to do it and determine its level of difficulty. This is similar to step one except you are taking all the COA's you developed and subjecting them to critical thinking to determine the feasibility, utility, and ease of each COA.

a. Walk up/downstream to find a ford
    a. If you look at a map of the area the terrain does not get much better than where this photo was taken.
    b. The river is in a very rough and undeveloped area.
b. Swim across towing a line for the rest of the party

a. It would take a very strong swimmer to get across a fast flowing river like this. Keep in mind that the water is cold so hypothermia becomes a consideration for whichever member of your party tries this. You will need to build a fire shortly after crossing and fires make smoke.

c. Use a log/raft to float across
   a. This is possible if you can find a suitable log close enough to the river. You also need to fabricate some kind of oar or pole to guide the log/raft or you will just drift off down the river.
d. Build a boat
   a. The same considerations as a log apply with the addition that you have to use some of your precious supplies to fabricate a boat.
e. Try and jump across boulder to boulder
   a. Is anyone a gymnast? This is an almost sure route to injury of at least one member of your party.
f. Throw a rope from one bank to the other
   a. This idea seems great in theory but can rapidly go wrong if attempted by the unskilled.

COMPARE COURSES OF ACTION

In this step you consider each COA and your analysis and then essentially determine an order of precedence for the considered COAs. You essentially conduct a debate over the pros and cons of the various COAs.

a. Walk up/downstream to find a ford
   a. This is feasible depending on time constraints.
   b. It presents the smallest risk of someone getting injured during the crossing
   c. It takes the longest with no certain prospect of success
b. Swim across towing a line for the rest of the party
   a. Feasible as long as there is a reasonably strong simmer in your party
   b. It should be quick

8

      c. The entire party will need to switch into dry clothes after crossing

c. Use a log/raft to float across
      a. Is there a log close enough?
      b. It takes quite a bit of time to fabricate and oar, get the log in the water, and get it to the other side
      c. The whole party and gear will probably not fit on the log/raft so some, maybe all, of the party will have to swim.
      d. Undoubtedly some portion of the party will need to switch into dry clothes after crossing

d. Build a boat
      a. Building an improvised boat is possible from the B.O.B. bag contents but it takes some skill
      b. Building a boat and an oar takes time
      c. The whole party and gear will probably not fit on the boat so some, maybe all, of the party will have to swim or more than one trip will be required.

e. Try and jump across boulder to boulder
      a. Depends on the availability of suitable boulders
      b. Very risky as the boulders are probably wet and slick
      c. The possibility of falling into the water and losing gear is highest
      d. Can be fast but can be slow if there is an accident

f. Throw a rope from one bank to the other
      a. Throwing is harder than you might think when the item to be thrown is attached to a line
      b. Might not fond anything suitable for use as a grapnel.
      c. Might not be able to get the line to snag on something secure enough on the far bank
      d. Party members will still have to go through the water to cross.
      e. Is more secure since all party members will have a line to grasp and avoid being caught by the current

DETERMINE A COURSE OF ACTION

Having considered the merits and drawbacks of all your COAs in the last step now it is time to make a decision. Generally you should make one decision with a fallback if your primary COA does not work. In the considered problem my decision would probably be to try option f first and if that does not work fallback on b. That is, I would try to fabricate a grapnel and toss a line across the river and if that does not work within some arbitrary time limit, say 30 minutes, then I would have the strongest swimmer go ahead and swim across. My COA order of precedence would look like this:

1. Throw a rope from one bank to the other
2. Swim across towing a line for the rest of the party
3. Walk up/downstream to find a ford
4. Use a log/raft to float across
5. Build a boat
6. Try and jump across boulder to boulder

IMPLEMENT THE CHOSEN COURSE OF ACTION

This step is simple. Keeping in mind all the constraints considered in previous steps execute your plan. Lastly, be prepared to change your plan on the fly if something unexpected happens. Even the most thorough planning does not catch everything that can happen. Chaos theory rules in every situation.

CHAPTER 2 – PREPAREDNESS KITS

"You hit home runs not by chance but by preparation."
Roger Maris (MLB Hall of Famer)

The two kits below represent ideal kits. They are called the Go To Hell (G.O.T.H.) Kit and Bug-Out Bag (B.O.B.). Each bag actually serves a very different purpose. The G.O.T.H. bag has the minimum of essential items that should let you make it for a day up to a week if the situation requires. It is very basic. The B.O.B. on the other hand, is supposed to contain everything you need to get the hell out of dodge and on your way to wherever you will obtain long-term shelter. The B.O.B. should actually contain everything you need to live off the land if that is your only option.

The G.O.T.H. bag is one you can keep in your car, office, garage, or anywhere else where you might need a bag of essentials and don't have access to your B.O.B. bag. The G.O.T.H. is for when everything suddenly goes to hell unexpectedly and you don't have time to get your more lavishly supplied B.O.B. bag. Your B.O.B. bag should be at home.

One of the most important things about any kit is that you **must** periodically inspect your kit and replace items that are too old or past their expiration date. This is especially important with First Aid items.

When packing either kit but especially your B.O.B. the way you pack is almost as important as what you pack. When packing your bag there are a couple of things to keep in mind. The first is to keep the items you will use most often in the outside pockets or pouches or near the top of the main compartment. The second is to put the heavier items in your bag as close to the bottom as possible, this lowers the strain on your back from carrying a ruck all day. Your back is going to ache for a while until you get used to and adjust to humping that heavy bastard every day and there is no need to make it worse than necessary. The last thing is try and keep your B.O.B. bag down to between 1/3 and 1/2 your body weight. Any heavier and you risk doing some permanent damage to the point where you won't be able to take care of yourself. Personally, I shoot for a target ruck weight of around 35-45 lbs. and I am 5'11" and 170 lbs. That monkey on your back gets real heavy after about 2 hours of foot-marching on roads much less humping cross-country. In the Army we called our rucksacks ticks because they just suck the life right out of you.

If both kits seem to be heavy on the ways to make a fire that is on purpose. In a survival situation, fire is your best friend. Not only will fire cook your food, it will more importantly keep you warm when it is cold and save your miserable life for another day. There is no such thing as too many different methods to make a fire.

GO TO HELL (G.O.T.H.) KIT

This compact kit can be carried in the car, on the boat, or in a small ruck/backpack while hunting, hiking, exploring, etc. Most of the contents will fit in an Army 7.62mm ammo can which doubles as a pot for melting snow and device with which to dig an emergency snow shelter. (However, if you can carry it, include a small shovel. It is far, far better than trying to use an ammo can.)

Carrying container

- [ ] US Army Surplus 7.62mm ammo can (can be purchased at local Army Surplus tore or online)

General Items

- [ ] 550 Parachute Cord (25 feet)
- [ ] Signal Mirror
- [ ] Matches (2 boxes)
- [ ] Magnesium Fire Starter
- [ ] Bic® Lighter
- [ ] 40 Alcohol prep-pads for first-aid & use as fire starters
- [ ] Compass (learn how to use)
- [ ] Tea Candle X2 (wrapped in aluminum foil)
- [ ] Paper and pencil
- [ ] Fishing line, hooks, split shot leads
- [ ] Pocketknife
- [ ] Money
- [ ] Garbage Bags (3 large size bags)
- [ ] Dental floss (It's strong and useful as thread for sewing, fishing line, or for lashing branches for improvised shelters.)

☐ Gardening Hand-Shovel (carried externally)

First Aid Kit (Recommended contents)

☐ Moleskin

☐ Sterile pads (2 x 2 and 4 x 4)

☐ Sterile Gauze

☐ Neosporin

☐ Band-Aids

☐ Aspirin

☐ First Aid Tape

Food & Water

☐ Water Filter Straw

☐ Iodine Water Purification Tablets

☐ Emergency Rations (3 day supply for one person)

Optional/Nice to Have Items

☐ Instant Soup or tea (3-4 couple packages)

☐ Camp Cup/Canteen Cup

☐ Emergency Wire Saw

☐ Emergency Tent

☐ Campfire starter sticks

All contents will fit in a US Army Surplus ammo can, I use a 7.62mm can that I have from long ago. It is waterproof and closes very securely. If there is extra room (there should not be) you can keep things from rattling in the can by wadding up some wax paper and stuffing it around the items. The wax paper stays dry and also doubles as a fire starter.

My G.O.T.H. Kit weighs 8.5 lbs. and the ammo can fits perfectly behind the back seat of my pickup.

G.O.T.H. Kit laid out before packing

G.O.T.H. Kit packed into ammo can minus filter straw and trash bags

BUG-OUT BAG (B.O.B.)

The B.O.B. Bag is what you have pre-packed and ready to go at all times in the event you have to grab your gear and bail with at least minimal notice. If you have a vehicle, boat, or other means of carrying gear they would allow much more flexibility in how much gear you can tote but let's face it, it's highly unlikely these modes of transport would be feasible for long. This list should be adjusted to take specific variables of terrain and climate from your expected location/area of operation into account.

An additional thing to keep in mind is that you **will** end up humping everything on this list on your back. Play with the contents of this list and methods of packing it so that the load is comfortable on your back. I would recommend that your ruck weigh no more than 1/3 your body weight, and even at that it will get very old, very fast. Humping a load like this is a young person's game. You need to train and practice carrying a load that weighs as much as you're B.O.B. so that when the day comes you are both physically and mentally prepared for the monkey that will be on your back for the foreseeable future.

A tip for packing is to try and have the heaviest items as low as possible in the ruck to reduce shoulder and back strain.

Rucksack & Clothing Items:

- [ ] Frame rucksack (I use a Large US Army ALICE Pack)
- [ ] Lightweight mesh bag (for wild food gathering)
- [ ] Leather and Gore-Tex waterproof hiking or military style boots (will be wearing)
- [ ] Moisture-wicking inner socks (4-pair) (will be wearing additional pair)

- [ ] Wool outer socks (4-pair) (will be wearing additional pair)
- [ ] Wool Watch cap
- [ ] Boonie hat (will be wearing)
- [ ] Bandanas (3)
- [ ] Ripstop BDU pants (3 pair) (will be wearing one pair)
- [ ] Ripstop BDU long-sleeve shirt (3 each) (will be wearing one)
- [ ] Synthetic long underwear (2 pair)
- [ ] Gore-Tex™ rain pants and Parka
- [ ] Heavy-duty belt (military style Riggers belt)
- [ ] T-shirts (4) (will be wearing one under outer shirt)
- [ ] Synthetic long underwear shirt (2)
- [ ] Long-sleeve fleece jacket(1)
- [ ] Camouflage poncho (doubles as small tarp, and useful to hide unattended gear)
- [ ] Camouflage Poncho liner (perhaps the most useful item the US Army ever invented)

Shelter & Fire

- [ ] Camping hammock
- [ ] 550 Parachute Cord (minimum100-feet, more can be carried if you get creative about stowing it)
- [ ] Synthetic sleeping bag rated for the climate and season
- [ ] Ground Mat
- [ ] Pillow (A small camping pillow as there is no reason to be more miserable than you have to be)
- [ ] Emergency Tent

☐ Bic™ disposable butane lighters (Minimum 6)

☐ Magnesium Fire Starter (2)

☐ Fire Sticks (12-pack)

☐ Small bag of cotton balls soaked in Vaseline (tinder)

☐ Small roofing nails (small bottle of 100 or so)

Food & Water

☐ 3-day supply of Mainstay™ or Datrex™ emergency rations, or MREs.

☐ 1 gallon Ziploc™ bag of high-energy trail mix (dried fruits, nuts and seeds)

☐ Power bars (half dozen)

☐ Beef Jerky (several small packages)

☐ 1 gallon Ziploc bag of whole-grain oatmeal

☐ Small quantity of seasoning sauce (I use red Tabasco)

☐ One quart Nalgene bottles or Military Canteens, for drinking water (2 minimum)
[I personally carry two 1 quart canteens and a two-quart canteen, but then I think you can never have enough water]

☐ Iodine Water Disinfectant tablets (minimum 2 bottles)

☐ Water Filter Straw, I recommend the LifeStraw™ (2)

Hunting & Fishing

☐ Take-down .22 rifle

☐ .22 ammo (2000 rounds minimum)

☐ Colt 1911A1 .45 ACP clone or original (can't be beat for sheer stopping power)

- [ ] Holster for pistol to carry in accessible location
- [ ] Extra magazines (minimum 5)
- [ ] Carbine/Assault Rifle (optional, depending on situation)
- [ ] .45 ACP ammo (500 rounds)
- [ ] Selection of assorted fishhooks for bream up to large catfish
- [ ] Spool of monofilament line
- [ ] Spool of trot line for drop hooks
- [ ] Pre-made wire snares for small game (.o14" Piano Wire)

Tools

- [ ] Quality 18 to 24-inch machete with sheath
- [ ] Machete
- [ ] Fixed blade knife (I use an M7 Bayonet that fits the lug on an AR-15/M-16)
- [ ] Knife Sharpener
- [ ] Multi-tool (Gerber or Leatherman, it doesn't matter as long as it is good quality)
- [ ] Small mill file
- [ ] Diamond sharpener
- [ ] Hand-bearing compass
- [ ] Watch
- [ ] Maps of your operational area
- [ ] Stainless steel 4-quart cooking pot (with lid, handle removed)
- [ ] Stainless steel spoon
- [ ] Sewing Kit
- [ ] LED Crank flashlight

Miscellaneous

- ☐ Mosquito net
- ☐ Insect repellant with DEET
- ☐ Small tube of Sun Protection Factor (SPF) 50 sunblock
- ☐ Sunglasses with retainer and case (if traveling by water or open country)
- ☐ Basic First Aid supplies, bandages and antibiotic ointment
- ☐ Snakebite Extractor Kit
- ☐ Cortisone cream (for poison ivy, etc.)
- ☐ Benadryl (for bee and wasp stings)
- ☐ Imodium (Anti-diarrhea)
- ☐ Ibuprofen pain capsules (Ranger Candy, it is called)
- ☐ Field guide to edible plants (region-specific)
- ☐ Passport/driver's license
- ☐ Cash plus gold or silver coins
- ☐ Toothbrush
- ☐ Small bottle of concentrated anti-bacterial soap
- ☐ Small amount of tightly-packed toilet paper *(Leaves really suck)*
- ☐ Comb
- ☐ Pocket solar AA battery recharger unit
- ☐ L.E.D. version of the Mini Maglite, with extra AA batteries
- ☐ (Or small L.E.D. headlamp that runs on AA or AAA batteries)
- ☐ Small quantity of duct tape

☐ Small bottle of gun oil/multipurpose oil

If you have anything that takes batteries try to get all equipment that uses the same type of battery, preferably AA. Then you can purchase rechargeables and a portable Solar Panel battery recharging station. This will help ensure that it will take a long time before all your electric gadgets turn into strangely shaped rocks because you don't have any batteries for them anymore.

LIGHTWEIGHT FIRST AID KIT

This is a suggested list for lightweight field First Aid kit. I highly suggest adapting it to your needs but it is a good place to start from. It is important that you carry only those items that you know how to use and that you periodically check your kit and restock and replace old, expired medicine and worn items. If you can get your hands on one, a German spec vehicle First Aid kit has everything you will need to deal with major and minor trauma and is fairly compact. You can get one online from Bavarian Autosport for $29.95 or just do an Internet search for AutoVerbandkasten.

Basic Items

☐ 3-4 Sterile gauze pads (4" x 4")

☐ 2 Rolls of 4" wide sterile gauze

☐ 8 Band-Aids™ (Include a couple large-sized Band-Aids™)

☐ 6 Butterfly bandages

☐ 2 Triangular Bandages (Useful for slings and lashing to improvised splints)

☐ Min. 2 ea. 4" Israeli Field First Aid bandage

☐ Combat One-hand Tourniquet

☐ EMT Shears

☐ 1 Roll of athletic tape

☐ 1 small package super absorbency tampons without applicator (these are excellent for plugging bullet and puncture wounds)

☐ 1 Small bottle of tincture of benzoin (for cleansing wounds)

☐ 1 Tube of Neosporin or Providone-Iodine ointment (to dress wounds)

☐ 2 Pieces of moleskin, 4" x 4" (Minimum Qty.)

☐ 1 Elastic wrap (4-6" wide)

☐ SAM splint

☐ 20 Safety pins

☐ 1 bottle Pain killers (Aspirin, Ibuprofen, or Acetaminophen)

☐ Benadryl (antihistamine tablets)

☐ Pepto-Bismol tablets

☐ Any special medicine you need to carry. (Heart Medicine, Insulin, etc.)

☐ 1 Pair of tweezers (tweezers are also available on Swiss US Army knives)

☐ 1 60 cc Syringe (For suction of vomitus or irrigation of wounds)

☐ Minimum 10 pair of sterile exam gloves

Other Items You May Want to Consider:

☐ Microshield™ (lightweight mouth shield for giving CPR)

☐ 1 oz. Syrup of Ipecac (To cause vomiting in the case of poisoning. Know when & when not to use.)

☐ Charcoal Suspension (To absorb poisons remaining in stomach)

☐ Silvadyne™ (a water-based burn ointment)

☐ Cavit™, 6 gram tube (temporary filling material for lost fillings)

CHAPTER 3 – OUTDOOR SURVIVAL

"If you're seeking to survive in the wilderness then good gear will get you to the last 10%. Training and practice are needed for the other 90%."

Unknown

Living off the land is not as simple as going all Grizzly Adams with a beard and a mule. It is also not as simple as just killing whatever animal you want and eating it. There is a reason why pre 1850's or so most societies were full of sickly people who generally died by the time they were in their mid-thirties and a lack of modern medicine was just one of many reasons.

Hunting, fishing, and foraging is hard work but just doing what you need to do to survive aside from providing something to eat is hard work as well. There is more to know about just plain survival than most people ever thought about because we take so much for granted in modern society. This book just touches on the most important aspects. There is much more to learn than is contained in these pages.

HYGIENE

Basic sanitation /hygiene, hereafter just hygiene, is one of those things that most people do not even think about anymore because they don't need to. It is also something that I have not really seen too many survival books or blogs talk about and I don't know why. If people think of hygiene at all it is of the keep hot foods hot, cold foods cold, and wash your hands after going to the bathroom type. Those things are important but in a survival situation there are several other things to keep in mind as far as hygiene goes. Poor hygiene can be just as deadly, and more painful, than any accident or injury. If you don't pay attention to hygiene in a wilderness/survival situation it can kill you. Hygiene is much more than just keeping clean.

Most people are unaware that World War I was the first war in recorded history in which more soldiers died of battlefield wounds and their complications than from disease. Diseases such as Cholera, Typhus, Malaria, Amoebic Dysentery, Smallpox, Hepatitis, and Yellow Fever have historically been the main killers of not only soldiers but people in general. It is only the advent of modern public and personal hygiene that has made these diseases largely historical footnotes. Yet even today, these diseases pop up when hygiene services are disrupted after natural disasters. In 2005 in the wake of Hurricane Katrina despite the massive resources dispatched to the disaster area there was a small outbreak of Norovirus, which causes dysentery like

Good hygiene can save your life just as much as poor hyguene can TAKE IT

symptoms.

Hygiene covers everything from where you put your latrine, how you cook and handle food, how you treat cuts and scratches, to how often you brush your teeth.

PERSONAL HYGIENE

First, Personal cleanliness. The saying goes that cleanliness is next to Godliness and it is true to an extent because while God may save your soul, keeping clean will save you from getting sick from a stupid, avoidable illness. Face it, if you have to live in the woods for any length of time you are going to be dirty, your clothes will be dirty, your hands and face will be dirty, your whole body will be dirty, it is part and parcel of the roughing it experience. In some ways this is good. If you are dirty you will smell like everything else around you making it harder for you to be tracked by animal predators or other humans by your smell. Believe me, you can smell contemporary soaps and shampoos a long way in the woods because the smells are so unnatural. Just because you will be dirty does not mean you have to be filthy, and you don't want to be.

There are a few key areas of your body to keep clean and they are your hands, teeth, feet, face, armpit, and crotch in that order. If you keep those areas clean you can avoid most of the sicknesses that come along with being dirty. The most important of those are hands, teeth and feet. Hands because that is how you feed yourself, teeth because untreated cavities suck, and feet because that is how you get around.

I shouldn't have to say keep your hands clean but it is unreal how many guys and even some women revert to caveman and stop staying clean without prompting in the field. Keeping clean is work and it never ends. It always seems that as soon as you get clean you are dirty again, and you are. Of particular importance is to wash your hands before you eat or prepare food, each and every time. Brush your teeth after every meal, even if it is only with a frayed green twig.

Take care of your feet, make sure you air them out daily and change socks frequently, especially if you move a lot. Not only will changing socks help you in avoiding blisters, it will also help with avoiding athlete's foot, which can get very painful if left untreated. If I had to make a choice between another pair of pants and a few more pairs of socks in my bag the hands down winner would be socks.

To clean the other areas, armpit and crotch, you can do the same thing they do in hospitals, a sponge bath. You do this by using a wet or damp rag/hand towel and washing those areas. You want to do this at least once every day or two. If you don't you risk catching lice, which while not deadly in and of themselves, carry disease and itch like mad. Soldiers used to make games of catching lice off their uniforms during downtime and delousing was a ritual every time soldiers came off the front line. You don't want to do this because once you catch lice they are almost impossible to get rid of without burning your clothing.

Essentially, keeping yourself as clean as possible should become a daily ritual. When I was in the field it was always one of the things I did before I racked out for the night because you never knew if you would have time to do more than pee in the morning before you had to go somewhere or do something and sometimes you had to wait for even that.

As far as clothes go, not only should you change socks frequently, you should also change your underclothes at least daily. Washing your outer clothes should be done as often as practical but if your pants are a dirty you can survive for a week or so before changing them for clean ones. An old US Army trick is to always have a pair of socks inside your jacket or in one of the outer pockets of your ruck. That way you can change socks when you get a short break and tie the ones you were wearing off to the outside of your ruck to let them dry.

Remember, in a survival situation you are not going to have access to washers and dryers so you have to pay special attention when you do wash your clothes and repair any rips or tears as soon as possible to keep them from getting bigger. **What you have with you is all you will have for a while so you have to take care of your gear. If you take care of your gear, it will take care of you.**

FIELD SANITATION

There are two aspects of field sanitation that will concern you in a survival situation; food preparation, and waste disposal. Preparing your food properly will keep you from getting ill with any foodborne pathogens and proper waste disposal avoids attracting unwanted wild animal guests and keeps you from getting any of the diseases that were endemic before the advent of modern municipal waste disposal.

FOOD PREPARATION

The key things to remember when preparing food in a survival situation is anything you cook, cook all the way and any things you don't cook, wash thoroughly with clean water before eating it. Whenever possible you should cook your food as this definitely destroys the most common disease causing organisms.

That means that if you catch and cook game, cook the meat until it is well done. You don't want to get dysentery because you ate that piece of rabbit that was still a little pink. See the table in Appendix C for some of the illnesses from wild game that all fall under the general heading **Food Poisoning**. The most common foodborne illnesses are Salmonella and E Coli; both of which can be avoided by thoroughly cooking your food.

When I say wash uncooked foods thoroughly with clean water I mean wash it with water that has been boiled. There is no more foolproof way to ensure your water has no bacterial or viral contamination than to boil it for a minimum of one minute. If you wash your uncooked food with un-boiled water do not be surprised when a member of your party gets ill. Most sources of water have some pathogens in them. The smart thing to do is assume all water you did not treat yourself has bacterial or viral contamination.

When you do cook game, eat it while it is still hot. Not burning your mouth hot, but not lukewarm either. As soon as cooked food starts cooling down its pathogen load increases by the minute, which means the cooler it is the higher the likelihood you will get ill.

Ensure you purify all water you drink and the water you do your ablutions with. It makes no sense to purify all the water you drink but get sick from the untreated water you used to brush your teeth. That includes the water you rinse your toothbrush off with and what you do your dishes in..

In Iraq, we could not get this through the Iraqi trainee's thick skulls. They would drink the bottled water but continually used the non-potable shower water to brush their teeth with. On any given day between 5-10% of our trainees spent more time on the toilet than in class because they had diarrhea. We even had some trainees we had to Medevac because their diarrhea got so bad.

Use only purified water for drinking, hygiene, and washing anything you put in your mouth. Non-purified water is fine for showers and general equipment cleaning. Assume all water you find is impure and act accordingly.

The steps and methods of purifying water will be covered in more detail in the next chapter.

WASTE DISPOSAL

This next discussion is semi-disgusting but absolutely imperative to have. That is waste disposal. Not just trash, but animal leavings and of course, human waste. There is a US Army adage that goes; *"never shit where you live and eat."* That is sound advice and is the heart of any discussion of field waste disposal. Waste disposal is not just concerned with excrement however, it is also concerned with how to dispose of trash such that neither animals nor other people are attracted to your location. One of the biggest giveaways to your location that is avoidable is trash.

There are a few rules of thumb to always follow when it comes to waste disposal.

1. Never simply toss trash, bury it or pack it with you.
2. Never urinate or bathe upstream from where you get your drinking water.
3. Never bury solid waste (excrement/food waste) inside your campsite.

If you follow the above three rules you cannot go far wrong. Proper waste disposal helps to keep you healthy and hidden, both good things.

First, trash disposal. Trash is everything left over when you do any activity. It can be wrapping or packaging to discard, wood shavings, ashes from your fire, to the offal left over after you butcher an animal or fish. There are a couple of negative consequences for failing to dispose of your trash properly. Biological trash can breed disease and attract flies that carry disease. It emits a distinctive odor upon decomposition that attracts people and animals and it acts as a location marker for you.

The simplest way to dispose of trash is burn it. You have to be careful here with some things though. Plastic reeks when it burns and the smell carries forever if there is even the slightest breeze. Plastic also never burns completely so the best policy is not to burn it in the first place. Other trash such as food leavings, offal, paper, or combustible packaging should be burnt. That saves you the trouble of digging a separate trash pit and makes your campsite easier to conceal when you leave it. Plastic trash can be carried until you have enough to fill a small bag for burial. If you have MRE's in your ruck about an MRE bag worth of plastic trash is a good amount for burial.

The alternate method of disposing of trash you either can't or don't have time to burn is to bury it. Bury trash at least 2 feet deep to avoid having animals dig it up. Just because you can't smell it does not mean a coyote, bear, or raccoon can't. Don't bury it inside your campsite either. Bury trash at least 300 feet downstream or downhill from where you will get your water if there is a water source you are using.

Non-excrement waste is fairly simple to dispose of. Excrement is another story entirely. You have to be careful about what and where you dispose of such waste. Every guy knows the joy of standing next to a tree, whipping it out, and relieving oneself. Don't do it in your camp because flies and other insects congregate around urine too. Solid waste can present even more of a challenge as not only does it attract flies and insects, it can attract larger animals as well that can be pests or dangers.

For urination you want to go away from your campsite and downslope. The site should be no less than 150 feet away from where you will be eating or sleeping. Don't urinate into any water that you may use for drinking regardless of how tempting it is to listen to the splash.

There are two methods for getting rid of solid waste. The first is a cathole and the second is a slit trench or trench latrine. A cathole is fastest and the easiest to use when you are on the move or will only be in a given location for less than a week. If you will be somewhere for more than a week a latrine/straddle trench is the way to go.

Both catholes and latrine trenches should be at least 300 feet away from your campsite. Ensure they are downslope, you don't want a turd floating into your tent if you get a lot of rain. They should also be at least 300 feet from your water source and downstream from where you plan on getting your water if your water source is a creek or river.   Lastly, if possible try to place your latrine trench downwind from your campsite based on the prevailing wind in your area, latrine trenches stink regardless of what you do with them.

To dig a cathole you simply dig a small hole approximately 10 inches wide by about 6 inches deep. A handy yardstick is make it a circular hole as wide and as deep as an e-tool blade. If the ground is soft you can use the heel of your boot for this, if not, use your e-tool. Do your business into the hole, throw your toilet paper in and then re-cover it. If you are trying to be stealthy ensure that you return the ground as close to its original appearance as possible by sprinkling leaves and dry dirt over the hole.

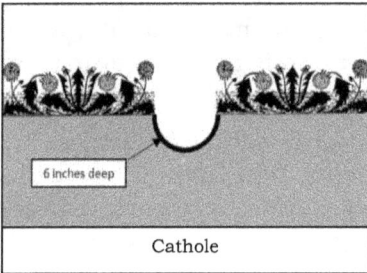

6 inches deep

Cathole

A latrine trench is slightly more complex but the principle is the same. It is important that you site your latrine trench properly taking into account the elevation of the trench in relation to your campsite, the location of water sources, and the prevailing wind. The trench will stink and if it is too close to your water source you risk contamination and the illnesses associated with untreated waste.

A latrine trench is a simple trench dug 10 inches wide, 6-36 inches deep, and 3-5 feet long. If the soil is amenable and easy to dig go for the maximum depth of 36 inches as this will help keep the smell down. Keep the spoil from digging the trench in a pile just off to the side of the latrine trench. The trench should be just wide enough that a person can squat down straddling the trench without great difficulty. You can also get creative in devising seats or seating arrangements for greater comfort. I suppose you could put magazines nearby in Ziploc bags if you really wanted to go all out. I have seen some crazy contraptions put up for seating on a latrine trench. If desired you can also build a screen out of available materials for privacy. A wise Vietnam vet I had as my first platoon sergeant once told that *"the mark of a real man is being able to take a dump in the middle of a busy camp and not worrying if someone is looking while they wipe their ass."*

Once you have your trench dug and amenities built, the trench is ready for use. You simply straddle the trench and squat down or alternatively get comfortable with a magazine and coffee and take care of business. As with a cathole, throw your toilet paper into the hole and then use the dirt from the spoil pile to re-over the section of trench you used. Covering the waste completely will greatly reduce

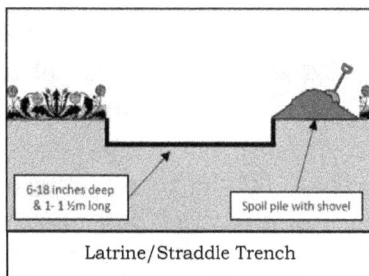

6-18 inches deep
& 1- 1 ½m long

Spoil pile with shovel

Latrine/Straddle Trench

the odor from the trench and you can also sprinkle cold ashes from a campfire on the waste prior to covering to stop the odor even farther. The trench can be reused almost indefinitely by extending it when it is about half full. Keeping in mind that the extensions must stay within the limits set by your siting criteria for a latrine trench in the first place.

Lastly, even if you are on the move, **always cover your waste**, especially excrement. Not only is this just good practice as it reinforces a beneficial habit; there is no reason to make tracking you any easier than it has to be for anyone trying to follow you.

MOVEMENT

Movement through the woods is different than walking down a city street. Distance assumes a much bigger importance afoot than in a car or plane. Both these things should be apparent and blindingly obvious but they are not. Simply walking across wooded, uneven terrain is an art, especially if you want to be relatively quiet while doing so. Any fool can crash through the woods announcing his presence to all and sundry. That is not a particularly smart thing to do in an end of the world situation though.

Distance too can be deceiving. Modern man is used to thinking in terms of driving time when we think about distance. Thus 60 miles is roughly one hour in a car and we think nothing about driving such distances. Indeed, some people commute such distances and greater for work every day. Now stop and think how long it would take you to ride a horse or better yet, walk that far. On a horse that is a minimum of two days, yes days, hard riding and three to four days at a sustainable pace. On foot, you are talking about more like a week to ten days for that distance, if you are in shape.

To get an idea of how far horses can travel look at any map of the US that was largely settled in the frontier period. Now pick ten towns along a single road, or better yet rail line and measure the distance between them. The average is roughly 13 miles apart. Split that and you have the average distance a wagon could carry a load in one day's travel. That seven and a half miles is how far a farmer could take his loaded wagon to market, spend the night, go to market day, and then travel home the day after that. A three day trip to go 7 1/2 miles from home.

For foot travel consult a map of market towns in medieval Western Europe, the same rule applies. Another thing to consider is that the average marching distance of a

Roman legion was eighteen to twenty-two modern miles per day. The Legions marched on good roads too, roads that they built themselves expressly for marching troops upon. During the opening campaigns of World War I, troops on the Western Front marched an average of seventeen miles per day and then fought for almost ten weeks. Walking anywhere is by itself hard work, walking on unimproved terrain is even worse.

When all is said and done and you have walked where you need to walk and are ready to get some food and sleep you need somewhere to camp. This is also a survival question not just because of weather but because of considerations of stealth and detectability. It is not cowardice to find a good campsite that lets you see but not be seen, that is prudence. Only a fool announces himself in a survival/hostile situation.

MOVEMENT IN VARIOUS TERRAIN

Accept upfront that you will not move far by foot on any given day. In the aggregate, you can make some pretty good distance though. If you can make ten miles a day, that is roughly 300 miles a month and it would only take you ten months to walk from sea to sea in the US. Hopefully you won't have to do that though. In the wilderness, you might be lucky to make five miles a day and seven and a half miles is probably a more realistic estimate.

Terrain can be an enemy just like people can. It is more implacable too as while the earth will probably not actively try to kill you, it is unforgiving of thoughtlessness and stupidity. There will not be signs saying cliff ahead, fire danger, falling rocks, or subject to flash floods. To avoid danger and an injury that can kill you as surely as an enemy you must be able to read the terrain yourself.

To be honest, unless you are a mountaineer or experienced climber I recommend avoiding mountainous terrain altogether. It is far too easy to get seriously hurt or killed in mountainous terrain than a novice wants to admit. Weather is very unpredictable in such terrain and can change from beautiful to life threatening in a matter of minutes. Climbing is inherently dangerous and a hastily or improperly tied knot can be the death of you. Rockfalls and rockslides occur unpredictably and the opportunities to be ambushed skyrocket in such terrain. Getting trapped in a box canyon by hostile action or weather is a very bad thing indeed.

If you live in or cannot avoid mountainous terrain the time to get training and experience on how to move through such terrain is before you need it. The learning curve is too steep to try and survive in such terrain unprepared for its peculiarities.

The most important thing about moving through wooded terrain is to avoid trying to break brush unless you absolutely have to. If you have to hack a path you are leaving a bright shiny sign for anyone to see that you have been here. Wooded terrain also comes in several different types. The two most common types of terrain you will see in the continental US and mainland Europe are first and second growth forest. First growth forest is full of small bushes and weeds that can form an almost impenetrable wall. Think of a whole forest full of the kind of thickets you see at the side of roads. Second growth forest is more open because mature trees have started to choke out some of the understory of lower growing bushes and vines.

When walking through woods roll your foot from heel to toe as you walk. Not only is this a more natural gait, it also tends to avoid making sharp cracks as you break twigs underfoot while walking. Be careful of fallen trees as they can shift underfoot when you try to go over them causing a sprained ankle or worse. Also be wary when crossing streams as there may be submerged hazards that you cannot see.

The best thing you can do is go out and get experience in moving through the kind of terrain you are likely to encounter in a survival situation before you need it and when help is just a phone call away if you find yourself in a difficult situation.

SHELTER

The first thing to consider when selecting a campsite is where to camp. The next thing is what kind of shelter you will use. If you have a tent that is great, but what if your tent is lost or you did not have one to begin with? There are several methods to make shelter out of existing material. Shelters that are every bit as good as a tent and that even blend in with the terrain better than any tent ever made.

CAMPSITE LOCATION

Many factors must be taken into consideration when selecting a campsite location. The most important of which is not shelter from the weather or the proximity to water, firewood, game, or even latrine facilities, but security. All other considerations pale in comparison to security. Mainly because it does not matter how ideal your site is in relation to everything else if you are unnecessarily vulnerable to attack in your campsite.

An ideal position from a security perspective is one where you cannot be approached unobserved but from which you have a backdoor where you can escape unseen. **The ideal position does not exist**, as the one condition negates the other. The closest you will get to ideal is a position that lets you see all the easy ways to get at you while the less easy ways are slow and noisy and you have a method of egress that you can block to delay your attackers after you have left. I do not recommend caves as they are normally traps if your location is discovered.

An example of a near ideal position is one near a navigable waterway where you have a boat that you can leave on, or a hilltop with a steep wooded descent on one side but grassy, easy approaches on the other sides. You will not find these often, more often you will have to compromise and sacrifice some security in favor of egress. That does not mean that good positions are not to be found.

Merely adequate positions can also be improved upon to make them better, often with surprisingly little effort. The section in chapter 5 on defenses comes in handy for this purpose.

Avoid establishing a campsite near frequently traveled game trails. People are naturally lazy and will follow trails even when they know they should not. Camping away from trails helps avoid being discovered by pursuers and also helps lessen encounters with natural predators who stalk such trails for the obvious reasons.

A part of security is ensuring that your location is not subject to natural hazards. Do not establish a position underneath a cliff wall where loose rocks can fall on you. No positions in seasonal streambeds. Being woken up by a flashflood does not make for a good day. Flashfloods can be caused by storms that are over the horizon and that you never see, especially in desert areas.

Poison Oak

Poison Sumac

Poison Ivy

Learn the appearance and typical locations of poisonous plants, especially the most common. Poison Oak, Poison Ivy, and Poison Sumac, while not deadly unless you are allergic all suck to get. There are other plants that are injurious just by touching as well. The milk of Castor plants is poisonous if it gets onto any unprotected skin. Stinging Nettles are also unpleasant and can cause a fever if you roll in a patch of them. The rule of thumb for poisonous plants is *"leaves of three, let it be."*

After security the next most important factor is water availability, especially if you will be in the position for longer than an overnight stay. Water should be readily available and you should have at least a largely concealed route to and from your water supply. Running water such as a stream or river is even better and a spring is preferable to any standing body of water. When choosing your location remember that you should always get your water upstream from **any** sources of contamination and it should be treated before using it for drinking or food preparation.

Firewood and game availability only really come into play in situations where you will be in one place for longer than a few days to a week or longer. Shorter stay of 1-2 nights do not necessitate taking these long-term requirements into consideration during site selection. Firewood, especially dry firewood, is important in cold climates and during the winter months as warmth can then be the difference between life and death. In a forest dry firewood or at least tinder can always be found if you know where to look. A great place to find tinder is to get it from the inside of partially rotted deadfall. Every second growth forest has deadfall. The amount of such depends on when the last forest fire swept though and how the forest has been managed. Keep in mind that fires with wet or green wood produce smoke and odor that can give away your position. Another thing to remember is do not build a fire under a snow covered tree in the winter time as the heat generated by the fire can melt the snow causing it to drop on and extinguish your fire.

Finding Game is covered in the next Chapter. Proximity to game however is generally only a concern in the case of long-term occupation of a site.

Lastly, shelter. If you are looking for an overnight site the most important thing about shelter is to pick a spot to pitch your tent that is sheltered from the prevailing wind. The direction of the prevailing wind can be determined simply by looking at the trees. Trees generally lean away from the prevailing wind. If possible, try to find locations with natural shelter such as rock overhangs or thick pine groves. Waterproof shelters can be improvised from many naturally occurring materials if your tent is damaged or lost.

A poncho can also come in very handy to make a lean-to as well.

IMPROVISED SHELTERS

The easiest shelters to improvise utilize a poncho or a tarp. A lean-to made with a poncho is one of the simplest to make and only takes a minute or two to put up. A lean-to can be constructed using either a poncho or tree branches. If you use tree branches, pine branches work best as they shed water better than branches from leafy trees.

BOUGH SHELTER

A simple and easy shelter can be made using your handy e-tool and a convenient pine tree. First, find a suitable tree. Pine trees are the only trees really suitable for this type of shelter because their branches are so close together that they shed water very efficiently. Additionally, the tree should be at least 15 feet tall so that once you have it felled the shelter will be big enough for you to get all the way inside.

Once you have found a suitable tree you simply cut the tree off about midway between your waist and shoulder such that it falls with the top of the tree to the upwind side. Do not cut all the way through the trunk, you want it to fall so that the crown of the tree is still attached to the stump. You should only have to cut 2/3 to 3/4 of the way through the trunk and then you can push or pull the crown over to the side you need it while leaving it connected. Once the tree is down with the crown and stump connected take some of your 550 Cord and securely lash the crown to the stump for added safety.

After you have secured the crown and stump you can make your shelter. Starting at the base of the crown start trimming the inside branches between the ground and trunk so that you make a tunnel like opening. Trim the branches as close to the trunk as you can and save the cut branches. Once you have the interior hollowed out take the branches you cut out of the middle and use them to make a floor and if necessary you can weave them into the exterior of the crown for additional protection from the elements. Put your fire pit about 3 feet in front of the entrance to your shelter with a low stone wall opposite to allow the heat to reflect to the interior of your shelter.

A well-constructed bough shelter should stay usable for up to six weeks and if you do not sever the crown completely from the trunk it can last an entire season.

ROOT SHELTER

The principle of a root shelter is similar to that of a bough shelter except you use a tree that is already down and trim the exposed root ball to make a hasty shelter from storms and other inclement weather. This type of shelter is really only suitable for overnight or emergency use. You can however, use a sufficiently large root ball as a foundation to construct a larger shelter.

LEAN-TO

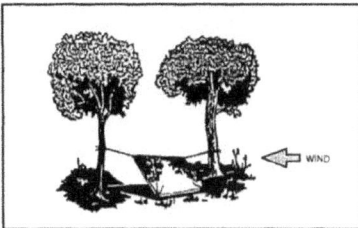

To build a lean-to with a poncho either find two trees roughly 8-9 feet apart and tie a piece of 550 Cord between them roughly knee high or you can alternately lash a wrist thick log to the trees with 550 cord for added stability. Then take your poncho or tarp and tie one of the long sides to the branch with about a foot of the poncho overlapping the cord. Take the other side of the poncho and stretch it out on the upwind side and then stake it into the ground. Once that is done take some leafy branches and stack them up on the sides to close it off making your lean-to a three-sided hooch. Build your fire pit in front of your lean-to with a wall opposite so that it reflects heat into the lean-to and you have a nice comfy improvised shelter.

CAVE

A cave can be used for both short and long term shelter. Caves can be improved greatly and made very comfortable with the added bonus that rock caves above a valley floor tend to stay dry in even the worst weather with only a little seepage. The biggest dangers from a cave are a rock fall that traps you inside or being tracked to your cave by an adversary. A good inspection of the cave should reveal if the rock is friable and liable to sudden collapse. You don't want to go too deep into a cave anyway as it is easy to get lost if you lose your light source or it breaks at which point you are going to be in a world of hurt.

Before you enter a cave make sure Smokey the Bear or some other animal did not get there first. Approach the mouth of the cave cautiously and look inside first. If it is inhabited you can drive the animal away by building a fire just outside the mouth of the cave and then throwing some green branches or leaves on it to smoke the animal out. Putting the fire just outside the entrance will tend to draw the smoke to the inside of the cave. Be sure to leave a way for the animal to escape because if you don't things will get very interesting, very fast, especially if there is a bear inside.

Once you get into the cave place your own fire pit near the back as natural air currents will tend to draw the smoke along the roof and out of the cave. It is advisable to fashion some sort of barrier by the mouth of the cave to discourage animals from either entering in the first place or returning to reclaim the house that you have evicted them from.

OTHER SHELTERS

- You can use a natural hollow in the ground as a base for a shelter but you must be careful or your shelter may flood when it rains.
- A large fallen tree can be used for emergency shelter if it has fallen such that one side provides protection from the wind.
- If no suitable trees are available you can use saplings that grow in row to

Sapling Shelter

make a frame or cut green branches yourself and drive them into the ground. This is also only a short term solution.

WEATHER

As we are all no-doubt aware the weather is notoriously difficult to predict, even for weathermen with all their modern equipment. There are a few things you can look for that signal weather changes. These are only rough guides but they can give you a heads up that a change in the weather is coming and give you time to prepare for storms or temperature changes.

You can determine wind direction by watching which way the treetops are blowing, dropping a few leaves or grass, or the old standby of licking your finger and holding it up. Wind direction lets you know which way to keep an eye out for approaching weather fronts. If the winds are shifting direction rapidly that means the atmosphere is unsettled and usually indicates a change in the weather is imminent. Often just before a storm blows in the wind picks up and blows very heavily with rapid direction changes. This is called a *Gust Front* and can give you ten to fifteen minutes warning of severe weather.

The way smoke acts can tell you something as well. Smoke that rises in a thin column generally means fair weather ahead while smoke that rises a little and then flattens out and spreads like layer means that rainy/stormy weather is coming in.

Birds and Insects often change their behavior in response to atmospheric changes that humans cannot perceive. Before it rains when the air is heavy and moisture-laden Birds and insects fly lower to the ground, this is often remarked upon about Swallows and Starlings. Flying in such a manner generally means that rain is likely. Insects are often more active before a storm, except for bees that are more active before fair weather returns.

Slow-moving or almost imperceptible winds and heavy, humid air are indications of a low-pressure front. Low-pressure fronts normally bring bad weather that will probably linger for several days. In a way you can "smell" and "hear" these types of front because the the sluggish, humid air makes wilderness odors more pronounced than when air pressure is higher Sounds are also sharper and carry much farther in low-pressure than high-pressure conditions.

Clouds come in a bewildering variety of shapes and patterns. A general understanding of the types of clouds and what they indicate can help predict the weather. There are four basic cloud types, all of which have Latin names.

1. Cumulus – means heap: these are the billowy clouds that people try to see shapes in on nice days in the park.
2. Stratus – means layer: these are the clouds that tend to cover the entire sky with a thin haze that weakens sunlight
3. Cirrus – means curl: these are the thin, wispy clouds you see high in the sky
4. Nimbus – means rain: these are dark, bulky clouds that bring rain or snow

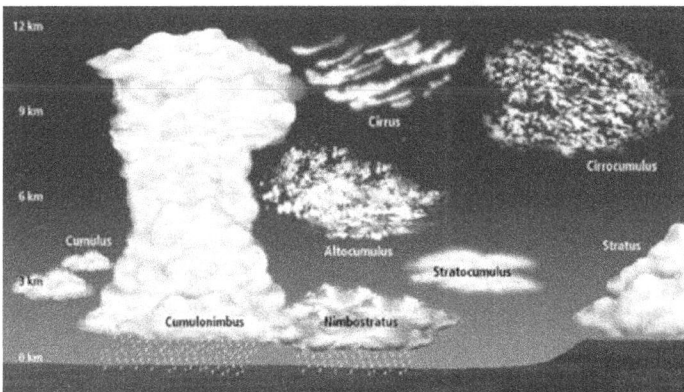

Cloud Types

FIRE

Fire will both keep you warm and cook your food. Plus, there is just an atavistic joy you get from sitting around a fire. A joy you cannot have if you cannot start a fire. The best way to start a fire is with your handy lighter, matches, or magnesium fire starter or Swedish Firesteel. Eventually you will run out of one or all three and then you need to start a fire the old fashioned Boy Scout way by rubbing two sticks together. Rubbing two sticks together gets old very fast though so there is an even better way using a bow and some tinder.

There are three different types of fuel for a fire and they apply regardless of how you start the fire. They are:

1. Tinder – Very fine, very dry material you use to get the initial flame going.
2. Kindling – Small pieces of wood used to build up the initial fire without smothering it
3. Fuel – The regular logs you put on a fire to build up the flame for cooking or heating and to maintain the fire.

You can almost always find some dry wood, even on the wettest day. The heartwood of old deadfalls makes good tinder when scraped out with a knife. Newer deadfalls only a season or two old is usually dry and easy to break for firewood.

To start a fire place your bundle of tinder in the center of what will be your fire pit and pile some kindling around it loosely enough that air can still flow freely. Then light your tinder and slowly feed the kindling to the fire until you have a good sized flame before adding fuel.

CAUTION

Never use sedimentary or river rocks for your fire circle or as warming stones as they can have moisture inside of them and they can EXPLODE when they get hot enough.

A couple of things to keep in mind before building a fire is to ensure that you use a fire pit or fire circle. A fire pit is nothing more than a hole in the ground roughly 1/3 bigger in diameter than the fire you want to build about 6 inches deep. Keep the dirt from digging off to the side so you can use it to smother the fire when no longer needed. A fire circle is made out of rocks and should also be about 1/3 bigger than the fire. With both types of fire you want to clear flammable material out of the area around the fire pit or circle a further 1/2 of the diameter as well to keep the fire from getting away from you. Always have a means at hand to put out the fire if it does start to get away from you.

There are a couple of ways to lay down a fire. Well actually more than a couple but two are the most useful; the Teepee and Log Cabin.

The Teepee fire is the best for concentrating the heat so that you can cook on it and get warm fast. The Teepee fire goes through fuel pretty quickly though and tends to not build a good bed of coals. If you need to heat up quick though this is the type of fire to lay.

If you only have a limited amount of dry wood or you want to build up a thick bed of coals the log cabin fire is the type to build. You stack your wood around the Teepee in this way to dry it out or stack it more tightly and let it burn to get a deep coal bed. This style of fire laying also burns a little more slowly so can be used if you only have limited wood supplies period.

Magnesium Fire-starter

Using a lighter is fairly straightforward but it takes a little knowledge to use a magnesium fire-starter or Swedish Firesteel, and even more knowledge to build a bow fire-starter.

To properly use a magnesium fire starter use a knife to shave some of the magnesium off the block into a small pile on top of your tinder. Once you have a suitable sized pile use the edge of your knife to strike sparks onto the magnesium from the striker rod until the magnesium catches fire. The burning magnesium should set your tinder aflame and from there you slowly feed the fire as described above until you have a healthy fire going.

A Swedish Firesteel is used in essentially the same manner except that it consists of only the ferrocerium striker rod with an attached striker.

The sparks from a Firesteel are struck directly onto your pile of

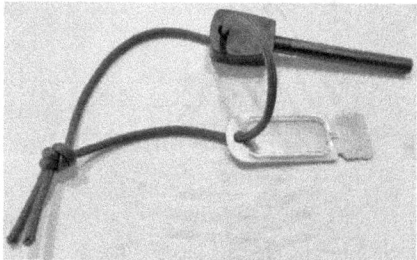

Swedish Firesteel

tinder instead of magnesium shavings. Ensuring your tinder is as dry as possible is very important if all you have to start a fire is a Firesteel as any dampness greatly increases the difficulty of getting your tinder to catch.

To make lighting your fire easier you can use an ancient method of making lighting a fire easier by making some char cloth beforehand. The use and manufacture of char cloth dates back to at least the ancient Romans and likely to earlier than that. Char cloth is made by placing any organic based cloth (cotton, linen, etc.) inside a can with a tiny air-hole and placing it at the center of the bed of coals from a fire. Let the can sit overnight in the coals. In the morning retrieve the can and open it. The cloth inside should be black and somewhat brittle. The resulting cloth can be used in place of magnesium shavings when starting a fire as it is burns much more easily than tinder alone.

Patrick J Shrier

CHAPTER 4 – MAP READING & NAVIGATION

"The world can doubtless never be well known by theory: practice is absolutely necessary; but surely it is of great use to a young man, before he sets out for that country, full of mazes, windings, and turnings, to have at least a general map of it, made by some experienced traveler."

Philip Dormer Stanhope (4th Earl of Chesterfield)

I remember hearing once while in the Army that a study was done that showed that 25% of all soldiers will never be able to read a map regardless of how much training they are given. My two years as a drill sergeant say that is false. Just about anyone can learn to read a map if they put the effort into it. That being said, map reading is a perishable skill that if you don't practice you will lose so you should get into the habit of taking maps with you anytime you go into the woods for any reason be it recreation or training and practice reading the maps you will actually use. Furthermore, you will not learn enough from this book to make you an expert; that takes practice and hands-on instruction from someone who is an expert.

There are actually two, maybe three kinds of maps you need to be familiar with. Road Maps, Topographic (Topo) Maps, and perhaps Nautical Charts depending on your location. Road Maps can be purchased online, at bookstores, and at just about every gas station. For the United States the best topo maps can be purchased from the United States Geological Survey (USGS) http://www.usgs.gov/pubprod/, they have maps providing

On USGS maps the contour lines are generally delinieated in feet above mean sea level instead of meters but the UTM Grids are in meters.

complete coverage of the US at varying scales.

Let's face it, in the era of GPS, Map Reading is a vanishing skill and in a survival situation the GPS satellites may not be up for long depending on the nature of the situation. If I were a foreign enemy one of the first things I would do is knock down the GPS network because it would hamstring GPS dependent weapons systems and platforms, and there are plenty of them from Navsets in vehicles to GPS guided bombs. Therefore, it behooves anyone preparing to be a survivor to learn to read maps and not depend that GPS will be there when needed.

I will only discuss Road maps and Topo maps while concentrating on Topo maps. Road Maps can be useful if you have to navigate long distances but if you are on foot they are generally less than useless as they tell you next to nothing about the nature of the terrain you will be walking across. Walking uphill is a lot different than driving uphill.

To start let's define a map. I have always found the US Army's definition to be concise and to the point: *A map is a graphic representation of a portion of the earth's surface drawn to scale, as seen from above.*

Below are two maps of the same area, Stottville, NY. One is a road map and the other is an extract of a USGS topo map. Notice the huge difference in the degree of detail

Road Map of Stottville, NY: Image courtesy Google Maps

between the two.

Unfortunately, you cannot distinguish the different colors of the map and topo maps are always printed in color because color lets the cartographer add more depth of detail and meaning to the marks and symbols on the map.

Road Maps are straightforward and should not require much in the way of explanation. Topo maps however, are a different story they contain many details about the land and the shape it takes as well different manmade and natural features that will affect your ability to move across it. This ranges from roads to cliffs to built-up area

s. All of this and more is repre sente d on a map.

Topographic Map of Stottville, NY: USGS Topograhic Map

KNOWING THE MAP

Before you can navigate with a map you have to be able to look at a map and make sense of what you see. The below section is the basic information you must know about a map to be able to grasp the basic information that a map conveys.

MAP SCALE

The level of detail to be found on a map depends on the scale to which the map is drawn. Map scale is always written on the map as a ratio of 1 to some other number and is written this way- 1:25,000 means a map scale of one to twenty-five thousand. Simply put scale is the ratio at which the things drawn on the map correspond to things on the actual ground. For example, if a map scale is 1:50,000 (the most common military map scale) that equates to features on the map being 1/50,000th the size on the map as they are on the ground. Going further for explanation on a 1:50,000 scale map a lake that is 1cm wide on the map is 50,000cm or 5km wide on the ground because it is 50,000 times larger in real life than it is represented on the map. Scale is difficult to explain in concept but becomes more easily gasped when you actually get on the ground and can see and experience the difference between a map representation and what is on the ground.

MARGINAL INFORMATION

The next thing is learning to read and interpret the marginal information on a map. The marginal information tells you everything you need to know about that particular map and the symbols used on it. This tells you not only the location the map represents but the identifier of adjoining map sheets, the age of the map information, and the particular symbols used on the map to represent manmade features. The marginal information will tell you how far apart in elevation the contour lines are as well as provide a declination diagram for the three Norths. Yes, I said three Norths. Topographic symbols are pretty much universal and will be discussed below.

First the Norths. There are three North seeking arrows on every topographical map that represent, true North, magnetic North, and grid North. True North is the actual direction to the geographic North Pole of the earth. Magnetic North is the actual direction to the earth's North magnetic pole, which is never at the geographic North Pole. Lastly, Grid North is the North that is represented by the grid lines on the map. For navigation purposes grid and magnetic North are all you are concerned with 99% of the time.

The three Norths on a map are represented by what is called a declination diagram that shows the three Norths and the difference between the two in both degrees and mils. The difference between grid and magnetic North is important when you plot a compass course because you have to compensate for the divergence between grid and magnetic North to get where you want to go. If you do not, you will end up lost. In a training situation you will get laughed at and in the real world you might get dead. It is important to keep in mind that the older your map data the more divergence in declination between Norths as the magnetic pole is constantly moving so it is important to try and update your declination data every 6 months or so to keep abreast of changes.

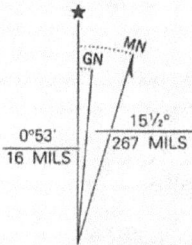

UTM GRID AND 1994 MAGNETIC NORTH
DECLINATION AT CENTER OF SHEET

Example Declination Diagram

COLORS ON A MAP & TERRAIN FEATURES

There are five basic colors on topographic maps both military and civilian and they are:

1. **Black**. Man-made features such as buildings and roads, surveyed spot elevations, and all labels.
2. **Red-Brown** (red on older maps). Cultural features, all relief features, non-surveyed spot elevations, and contour lines on red light readable maps.
3. **Blue**. Water and water features such as lakes, swamps, rivers, and drainage.
4. **Green**. Vegetation such as forests, orchards, vineyards, and parks.
5. **Brown**. Cultivated land on red-light readable maps.
6. **Other Colors**. Occasionally other colors may be used to show special information. As a rule, these are indicated in the marginal information.

In addition to the colors, terrain features are identified by the contour lines used to represent them. There are five major and three minor terrain features:

Major Terrain Features

1. Hill
2. Valley
3. Ridge
4. Saddle
5. Depression

Minor Terrain Features

1. Cliff
2. Spur
3. Draw

The easiest way to ID these are to use your hand as in the below illustrations taken from US Army FM 3-25-26.

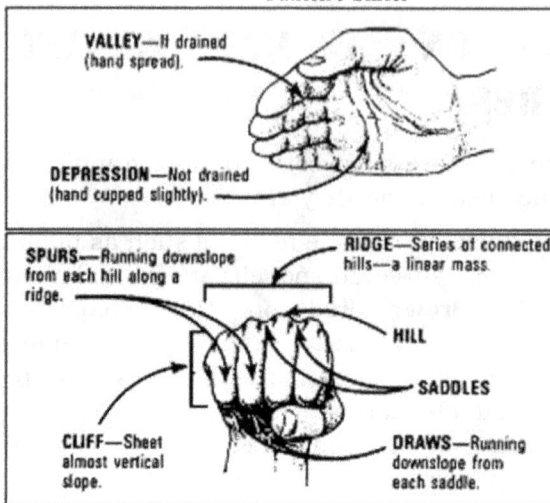

VALLEY—H drained (hand spread).

DEPRESSION—Not drained (hand cupped slightly).

SPURS—Running downslope from each hill along a ridge.

RIDGE—Series of connected hills—a linear mass.

HILL

SADDLES

CLIFF—Sheet almost vertical slope.

DRAWS—Running downslope from each saddle.

The way these terrain features are shown on a map is with contour lines. Contour lines are lines drawn on a map that correspond to a specific elevation above sea-level. The terrain features are defined and illustrated below using the images to be found in US Army FM 3-25-26 Map Reading and Land Navigation

Major Terrain Features

1.   Hill – A point of high ground characterized by the ground sloping downward in all directions.

HILL

2.   Valley – Fairly level ground bordered on three sides by higher ground. A valley does not necessarily have to have a water course in it. On a map, the U-shaped contour lines in a valley always point upslope.

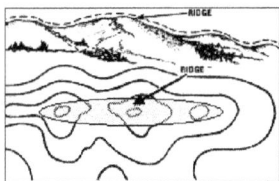

3.   Ridge – A ridge is a line of high ground. It is not necessarily a line of hilltops as it can be a long finger of land as well as a series of connected hilltops. On a ridge the land is level on two sides and slopes down on two sides.

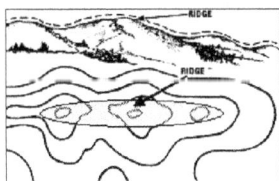

4.   Saddle – this is a dip or a low point along the crest of a ridge and can be a break in the ridge or the land between two connected hilltops. On a saddle the land rises on two sides and slopes down on two sides

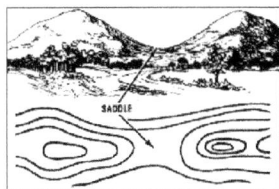

Depression – a depression is essentially the opposite of a hilltop. It is a low point or hole in the ground. In a depression the ground rises on all four sides.

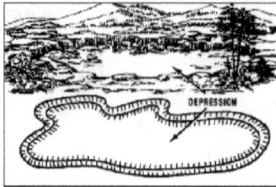

Minor Terrain Features

1.   Cliff – A cliff is a vertical or near vertical slope. It is represented by contour lines that come together to form one line or a single contour line with tick marks that point downslope.

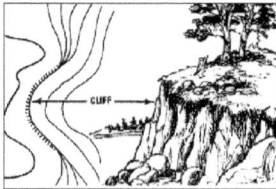

2.   Spur – A spur is a ridge's smaller cousin. It generally comes off a ridge or hill between two parallel streams of intermittent drainage channels.

3.   Draw – a draw is a valley's smaller cousin and is the furrow coming off a ridge formed by a stream or intermittent drainage channel.

In general the difference between a draw and a valley is you can drive a vehicle in a valley and cannot in a draw. The same distinction applies to ridges and spurs; a ridge will support a vehicle while a spur will not.

GRID LINES

Every topographical map is broken up into a grid of boxes. The lines that make these boxes are called grid lines and using these grid lines allows you to plot positions, including your own, and find the location of other features. Once you can do these two tasks you are well on your way to being able to navigate successfully. Every position on a map can be identified by the intersection of a north-south line with an east-west line, this is called the grid coordinates. The military uses a system called MGRS, which is closely paralleled by the system used by the USGS.

Both systems break a map down into grid squares that are 1000m on a side. Using a 4-digit grid-coordinate puts you inside a circle with a diameter of 1000m. Using a 6-digit grid makes that circle 100m and 8-digits makes it 10m. Prior to the age of GPS 6-digit grids were the standard and they will be again when GPS goes offline. If you cannot find a location once you're within 100m of it you should probably curl up and die and save yourself some pain.

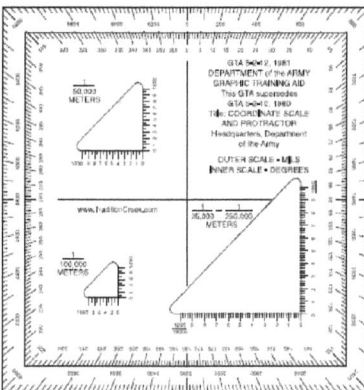

Military Style Map Protractor

Sometimes precision is a necessity when plotting points on a map such as when plotting out a compass course or recording the location of booby traps, mines, notable points, or equipment caches. An invaluable tool for determining more precise locations when working with a topographic map is a Map Protractor. There are civilian map protractors available or you can buy a military protractor at many places online or at local Army-Surplus stores.

To plot a location the key thing to remember is read a map **right and up**. Not the opposite left and down, not right and down or left and up but **right and up each and every time**. Failure to read **right and up** will get you lost every time. I will demonstrate the correct way to read a map in the below illustration.

To determine a 4-digit grid coordinate you simply read the number of the north-south grid line to the left of the position you want to plot and then add the number of the east-west grid line below it. In the below illustration the 4-digit grid coordinate for the black dot is **1383**

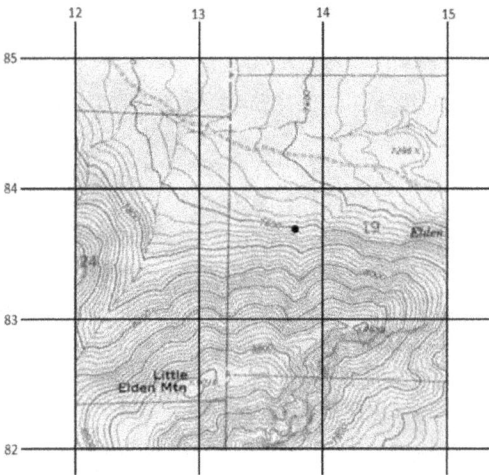

Determining a 4-Digit Grid Coordinate

To determine the 6-digit grid coordinate you simply imagine each block broken down into tenths and essentially guess, or you can use the proper scale protractor to determine it. An eyeballed 6-digit grid for the above point would be **138837** as shown below.

If the area you are operating in is extremely large you add the 2 letter 100,000 m² identifier to the grid. If that identifier were ED for the above 6-digit grid the grid would be **ED138837**. For even larger areas you identify the map sheet you are working from. All this is found in the marginal information of your map.

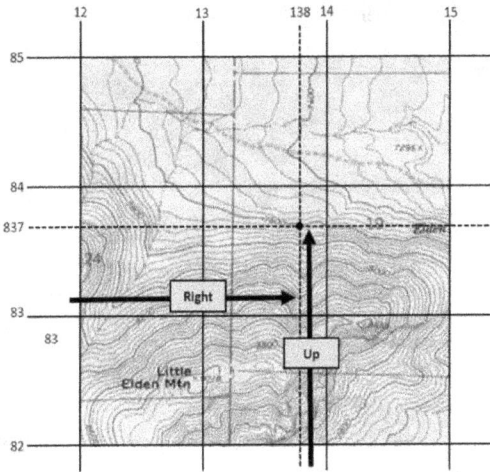

Determining a 6-Digit Grid
Coordinate

MAP ORIENTATION

Proper orientation of a map is a key task to successful navigation planning. This is no more than aligning the north axis of the map with actual north. There are two simple methods for doing this.

The first method is to use a compass to line up the edge of a lensatic compass with magnetic north on the declination diagram and turn the map until the north arrow on the compass and the magnetic north arrow on the map line up. Once you have done this your map is oriented to the terrain.

The second method is to orient your map with the terrain. This method is used if you are in a hurry or do not have a compass. To do this you must also have a general idea of where you are on the map. The first step is to pick two prominent terrain features you can see and locate them on the map. Once you have done that you turn your map until you can look at a terrain features on the map and then raise your head and see the same terrains feature on the ground. Now your map is oriented.

DETERMINING DIRECTION

Before you can do anything with or without a map you need to be able to determine which direction you are moving or facing. Hopefully you have a compass with you but if you do not there are several other methods for determining direction that do not require a compass.

COMPASS

A compass can be extremely useful if you know how to use it and an expensive paperweight if you don't. A compass is actually very easy to use but it is also easy to use one incorrectly and end up lost. The most common mistake people make when using a compass is not holding it level so that they get false azimuth readings.

Before you can use a compass you need to purchase one. I recommend you splurge and spend the $100-$150 to get a mil-spec lensatic compass with tritium dial. Not only are these great compasses, they are rugged enough that they will not break easily. It is well worth the expense to buy a good one. The best way to tell whether you have a mil-spec compass is to look at the top of the compass itself and see if it has the NSN, Manufacturer, and DoD Contract number embossed on it as in the above example. The paint should not be as chipped as mine but then again, I have had my compass since 1990 when I bought one because I was tired of always asking supply to get one for me.

There are five parts of the compass you must know. , The sight wire, sight glass, thumb loop, distance scale, and azimuth dial. You will use all parts when navigating or plotting how to navigate from one point to another. See

Sight Wire	Azimuth Dial	Sight Glass

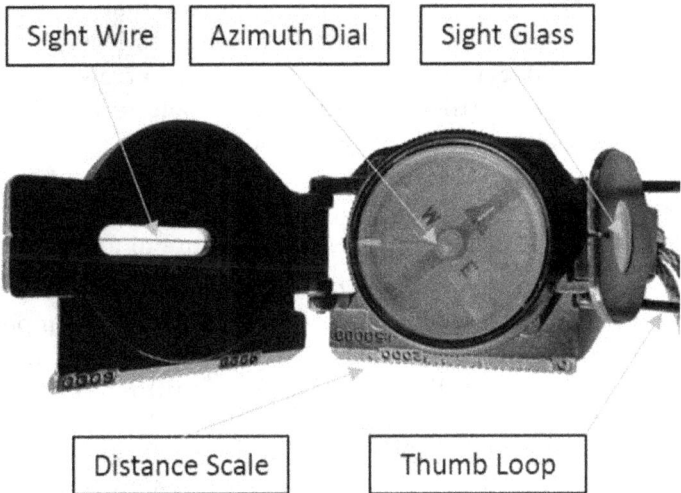

Distance Scale	Thumb Loop

illustration on the next page.

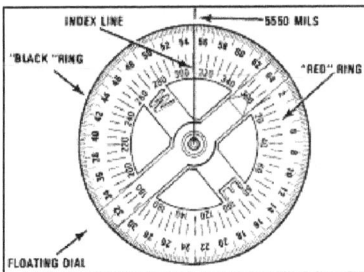

The azimuth dial of a compass consists of four parts. An index line, the floating dial, an outer black ring of numbers and an inner red ring of numbers. The outer black numbers are angular mils and the inner red numbers are degrees of arc. The index line is used to determine azimuth.

Let's talk about the difference between degrees and mils first. The mil is a NATO standard measure of angle and is pretty much only used by the military. There are 6400 mils in a circle and mils are used for things like adjusting artillery fire and estimating range. When sighting in armored vehicles. Mils allow for a more precise measurement of angle than degrees. There are roughly 17 mils in a degree. You will not use mils very much. Degrees are the standard that we learned in school. There are 360 degrees in a circle and for dismounted land navigation degrees work just fine.

The other part of the azimuth dial is the north seeking arrow. When you hold a compass level so that the dial can float freely the north seeking arrow will always point to the earth's north magnetic pole, always. That a compass only points to magnetic north become important when plotting a compass course on a map and will be explained in more detail later. For now, it will suffice if you keep in mind that a compass **only** points to magnetic north.

Now that you know what the parts of a compass are you need to know how to read one. To read a compass you point the sight line at the object you want to know the direction to and then read the azimuth. You read the azimuth by looking at the azimuth dial and reading the number that stands under the index line. That is the azimuth. In the illustration above the azimuth is 5550 mils or 310 degrees.

There are essentially two different ways to hold a compass to read an azimuth. The center hold and the cheek-to-thumb hold. The cheek-to-thumb method is normally used when navigating a compass course or to get a more exact azimuth when trying to determine a location using intersection or resection. The center hold method is used when following a general heading.

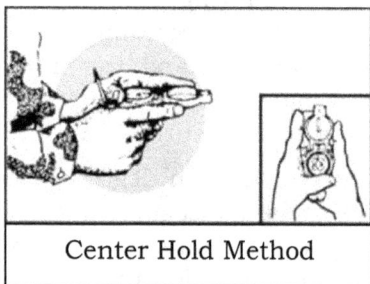

Center Hold Method

To use the center hold method put one thumb through the thumb loop of the compass and extend the fingers of that hand along the edge of the compass. Wrap the other hand behind the first hand extending those fingers along the other side of the compass. Then hold the compass level against your belly button and turn to face the object or location of the azimuth you are trying to determine. Once you are facing the direction you want simply read the azimuth off the azimuth dial.

The cheek-to-thumb method is used to determine a more precise azimuth to a specific object or location. This is done by placing the thumb of one hand through the thumb loop and grasping the compass with the fingers on that hand. Then move the sight glass such that it is at an angle of the azimuth dial. Once the sight glass is positioned move the lid of the compass until it touches and interlocks with the sight glass. Still

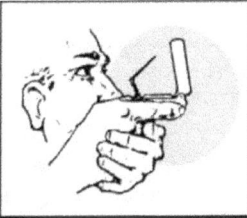

Cheek-to-thumb Hold Method

holding the compass move your thumb to your check until you can look through the notch above the sight glass and see your objective through the hole around the sight wire. Line the sight wire up with your objective and glance down through the sight glass to the azimuth dial and read the azimuth under the index line. These are the two most common and useful methods of holding a compass to determine the azimuth to a distant location or object. The other use for

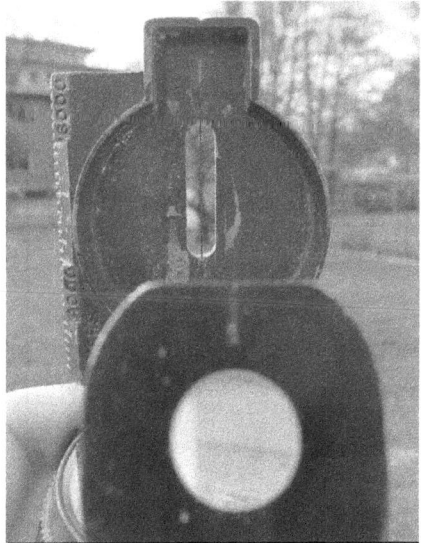

View when using the Cheek-to-thumb Hold Method

a compass is to unfold it completely and lay it on your map to orient the map but that is covered later in this chapter.

SUN & STARS

If you don't have a compass north can be determined using several other methods but these give you only a rough approximation at best. A rough approximation is better than total cluelessness though.

SUN

There are two very simple and easy methods of determining north if the sky is clear and the sun is shining. They are the stick method and watch method. Using the sun will always point you towards true north which is slightly different from magnetic north to a greater or lesser degree depending on where you are at in the world.

STICK METHOD

The stick method of determining north is simplicity in itself. It is time consuming but fairly accurate. To do this you need two sticks or a stick and two stones. One of the sticks must be as straight as possible with a thin tip. The longer the straight stick is and the thinner the tip the more accurate a reading you will get.

The first step is to find a location in full sun that is free of vegetation or

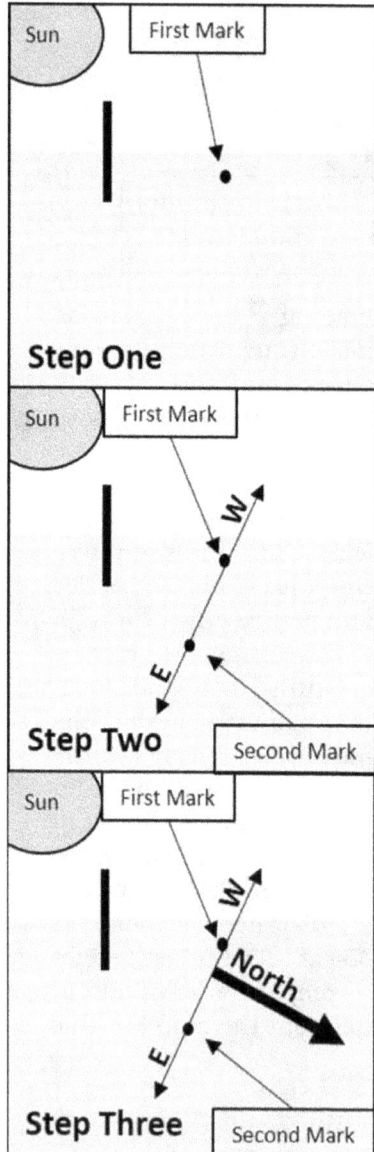

Step One

Step Two

Step Three

brush. Push the straight stick into the ground so that you can see its shadow clearly. Now mark the tip of the stick's shadow with one of the stones or draw an **X** at the shadow tips location. Next, wait for 15-20 minutes then mark the shadows tip again. The shadow will move from west-east regardless of where you are at on the earth. Once you have marked the two spots draw a straight line between them then stand facing away from the line you drew with your left heel against the first mark you made. You are now standing facing true north.

WATCH METHOD

If you have a normal wristwatch with and hour and minute hand that is set correctly you can quickly and easily determine true north using the face of your watch. The way to do his is to take your watch and looking at the face point the hour hand at the sun regardless of the time of day. In the northern hemisphere the point halfway between the hour hand and 12 o'clock on the watch is true north. In the southern hemisphere you do the

Watch Method

opposite and halfway between 12 o'clock and the hour hand is true north. At noon in the northern hemisphere the sun is always due south and in the southern hemisphere it is due north at noon.

STARS

You can also use the stars to find north. In the northern hemisphere find Polaris, the North Star. Polaris is the star at the end of the handle on the Little Dipper. If you cannot find the Little Dipper you can use the stars on the outer edge of the Big Dipper's scoop as pointers to find

Polaris. From the outer edge of the scoop on the Big Dipper draw an imaginary line from the bottom to the top and follow that line until it intersects Polaris at the end of the Little Dipper's Handle. From Polaris imagine a line straight

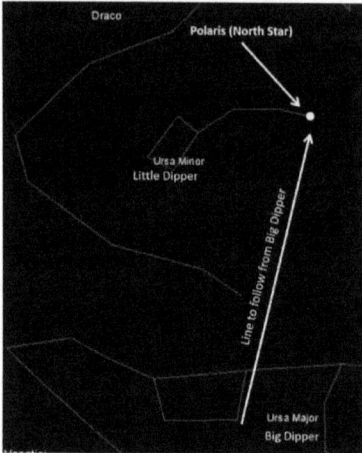

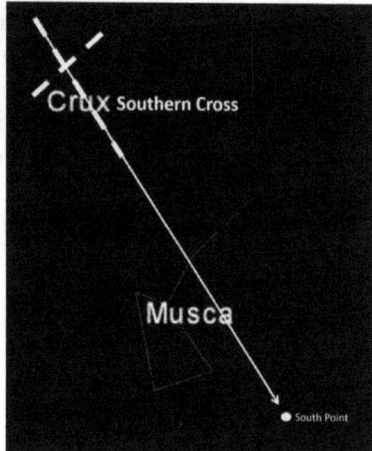

Finding the Southern Cross

down to the ground. That is North.

In the southern hemisphere there is no equivalent to Polaris. You can use the Southern Cross constellation however as a pointer to find south. This is a little trickier than using the North Star to find north. Crux is the name for the Southern Cross and it is made of five stars that form a cross shape. Form an imaginary line from the long axis of the Southern Cross and extend it towards the horizon for five time the apparent length of the constellation itself. That imaginary point is south. From the point drop straight down to the horizon to find South on the ground.

Finding the North Star

72

NAVIGATION WITH A MAP

It is not enough to be able to read a map, you must be able to use what you read. The main use is navigation and the below section provides the most basic techniques to allow you to read a map and get from one point on the ground to another.

DETERMINING YOUR POSITION

A map is worthless if you cannot plot your position on the map. Absent that ability you might as well use your map to start a fire for all the good it will do you. In order to determine your position on the map you must have a general idea of where you are at. The first thing to do is orient the map then you can use one of the following three methods to pinpoint your position on the map. Terrain Association, Intersection, or Resection. Terrain association requires nothing but a map and a Mark I eyeball while intersection and resection require a lensatic compass that you can shoot azimuth's with.

TERRAIN ASSOCIATION

Terrain association is nothing more than identifying some prominent terrain features in your vicinity and then finding them on the map. Estimate your distance from the various features and using that estimate locate your position on the map relative to the terrain features you have identified. The features you use do not have to be actual terrain such as hills or ridges you can also use man made features such as buildings, radio towers, intersections, etc. In fact, it is better to use man made features as they are more easily identifiable and are plotted with more precision on the map. The next method is more technically difficult but is still easy. Terrain association will only give you a rough approximation of your location on the map, generally within a few hundred meters, which is at least good enough to get you moving and you can continually refine your position estimate as you move and see how your selected features change their perceived position. In the end, it is only a rough guide though. To more precisely locate your position you must use intersection/resection.

INTERSECTION/RESECTION

Intersection and Resection use a compass, pencil, straight edge, and your map to get a fairly precise estimate of your physical location. A compass is not strictly necessary to accomplish either but it sure does make it faster and more accurate. Intersection is used to find the location of what you are looking at and Resection is used to find your own location.

The explanations below are taken almost directly from US Army FM 3-25.26, sections 6-7 and 6-8.

INTERSECTION

Intersection is the location of an unknown point by successively occupying at least two (preferably three) known positions on the ground and then map sighting on the unknown location. It is used to locate distant or inaccessible points or objects such as enemy targets and danger areas. There are two methods of intersection: the map and compass method and the straightedge method.

When using the map and compass method

1. Orient the map using the compass.
2. Locate and mark your position on the map,
3. Determine the magnetic azimuth to the unknown position using the compass.
4. Convert the magnetic

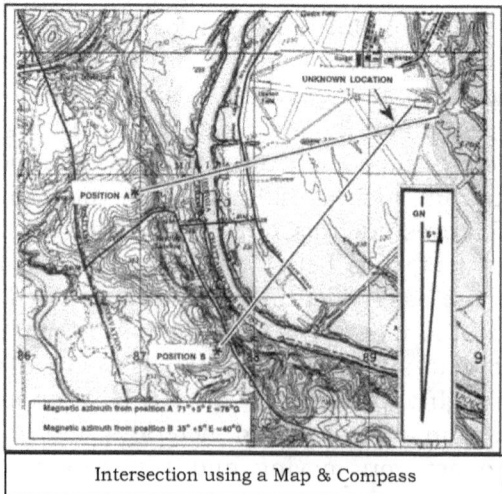

Intersection using a Map & Compass

azimuth to a grid azimuth.

5. Draw a line on the map from your position on this grid azimuth.
6. Move to a second known point and repeat steps 1, 2, 3, 4, and 5.
7. The location of the unknown position is where the lines cross on the map. Determine the grid coordinates to the desired accuracy.

The straight edge method is used when a compass is not available. When using it

1. Orient the map on a flat surface by the terrain association method.

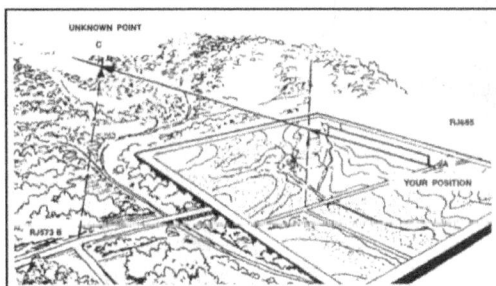

Intersection using the Straightedge Method

2. Locate and mark your position on the map.

3. Lay a straight edge on the map with one end at the user's position (A) as a pivot point; then, rotate the straightedge until the unknown point is sighted along the edge.

4. Draw a line along the straight edge
5. Repeat the above steps at position (B) and check for accuracy.
6. The intersection of the lines on the map is the location of the unknown point (C). Determine the grid coordinates to the desired accuracy

RESECTION

Resection is the method of locating one's position on a map by determining the grid azimuth to at least two well-defined locations that can be pinpointed on the map. For greater accuracy, the desired method of resection would be to use three or more well-defined locations.

When using the map and compass method—

1. Orient the map using the compass.
2. Identify two or three known distant locations on the ground and mark them on the map.
3. Measure the magnetic azimuth to one of the known positions from your location using a compass.
4. Convert the magnetic azimuth to a grid azimuth.
5. Convert the grid azimuth to a back azimuth by adding or subtracting 180 to the grid azimuth as appropriate. Using a protractor, draw a line for the back azimuth on the map from the known position back toward **your** unknown position.
6. Repeat 3, 4, and 5 for a second position and a third position, if desired.
7. The intersection of the lines is your location. Determine the grid coordinates to the desired accuracy.

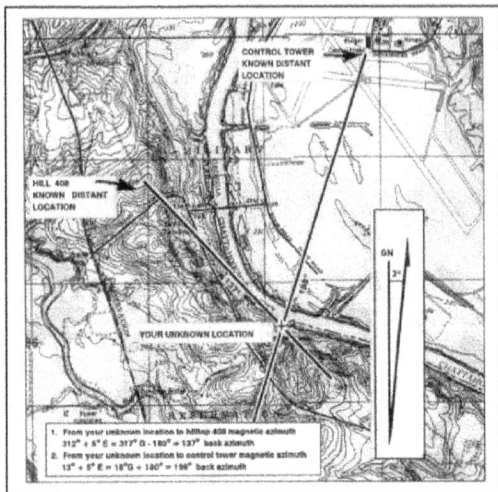

Resection using a Map & Compass

When using the Straightedge Method—

1. Orient the map on a flat surface by the terrain association method.
2. Locate at least two known distant locations or prominent features on the

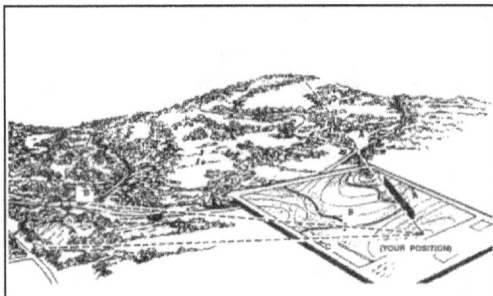

ground and mark them on the map.

3. Lay a straightedge on the map using a known position as a pivot point. Rotate the straightedge until the known position on the map is aligned with the known position on the ground.

Resection using the Straightedge Method

4. Draw a line along the straightedge away from the known position on the ground toward **your** position.

5. Repeat 3 and 4 using a second known position.

The intersection of the lines on the map is your location. Determine the grid coordinates to the desired accuracy.

PACE COUNT

One of the most important things when navigating on foot is to keep track of how far you have traveled. A simple and fairly reliable way to do this is by knowing your pace count. You want to know your pace count in meters because just about every topo map in the world is delineated in meters anymore because they multiply so much more simply and rationally than do inches, feet, yards, and miles.

Determining your pace count is simple and something you want to do before the end of the world. You want to determine your pace count on both level and uneven terrain because your stride changes walking up or down a slope than when walking on level ground. To do this simply mark out a straight line course a minimum of 100m long but preferably 300m long.

Once you have your course laid out start at one end and walk the length of it and back counting your steps as

---

For example if you took 156 paces walking a total distance of 600m then –
156 ÷ 6 = 26
Giving you a pace count of <u>26 paces per 100m</u>

---

you do. You can either count every time your foot hits the ground or every time your left foot or right foot hits the ground. Once you have walked the entire course and back using the number of steps you took divide that number by the multiple of 100m your course is. The answer is your average pace count for 100m.

Once you have determined your pace count you are set to start walking. However, it gets pretty old trying to keep count of your pace if you have to walk any appreciable distance. Thus GI's, being the eminently practical types that they are, came up with a pace counter or Ranger Beads to help them out while keeping a pace count.

This is nothing more than a length of 550 Cord with two different sets of beads or washers on it set such that they can be slid a short distance kind of like the scorekeeping beads on a foosball table. (See illustration). Generally one set has ten beads and the other five.

Pace Count Beads (Ranger Beads)

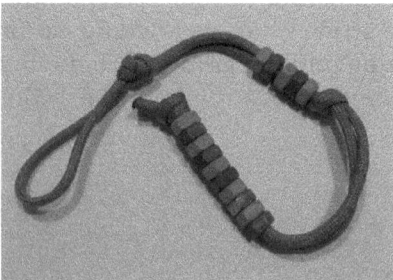

The way to use them is simple. While walking and counting paces, every 100m slide one of the beads on the set of ten to the end of its amount of play and do the same for every subsequent 100m until all have been slid to the opposite side. This is 1km. Once you have reached a km slide one of the beads on the set of five and then slide the ten back to where they were originally for the next km. You can do this for 5km before you must reset the beads.

NAVIGATING WITH AND WITHOUT A COMPASS

Now that can plot both your position and somewhere else how do you get there? You can either navigate using the terrain or you can follow a compass course. Navigating the terrain is simpler but less exact and for that reason tends to be faster as well.

You navigate by terrain in essentially the same manner that you orient your map with terrain. The difference is that when navigating by terrain you take note of what terrain exists between you and your objective and then walk over or around the intervening terrain using the terrain itself to ensure you are still on course. This can be easy in areas with no vegetation and gentle terrain or exceedingly difficult in heavy wooded areas or chaotic terrain.

Navigating by compass is more time consuming but also more exact than using the terrain alone. To navigate by compass you plot the azimuth to your objective or the intervening points and then follow those azimuths the plotted distances until you reach your objective. If you plot intervening points that are not on the straight line to your objective this is called dog-legging and is where many people get lost. There is a trick to navigating with compass in the woods or really anywhere. That trick is to always determine an azimuth and a back azimuth to two recognizable features on as straight a line as possible between your location and the objective.

Dog-legging a compass course almost never brings you out right on the objective because of slight shifts when you are walking the course due to terrain and vegetation. Once you think you are at your objective you can verify your position if you quickly determine the azimuth to both of your points. If the azimuths are correct then you are where you wanted to be. If they are not then it is a simple matter to consult your map and determine how far off you are. This is especially important if you are making a long move of 5km or more because the farther you travel the larger any navigation errors become.

Of course, if you get totally lost you can always determine your position once again using the methods described earlier and start over. The good thing is that with practice you become better at it until you reach a point where you think are so good you start making shortcuts, which is when you get lost all over again and become the butt of numerous jokes, especially if you have talked smack about your navigational abilities. Once you cross that hump and realize that it is always possible to err while navigating and take that into account you are on your way to becoming proficient.

If you have a GPS you can just plug in grids and set waypoints and away you go. That only works until the batteries die though and in a survival situation Energizer won't be making any more batteries If you have Ni-Cad Rechargeables the situation may not allow to recharge them and you are stuck doing it the old fashioned way. Technology is great but you must plan, even count on, technology to fail you at some point. A final piece of advice is to get a copy of the military Land Nav manual and practice, practice, practice! **Land Nav is a perishable skill!**

CHAPTER 5 – ACQUIRING FOOD & WATER

"Give a man a fish, feed him for a day: teach a man to fish, feed him for his whole life."

Lao Tzu (Ancient Chinese Philosopher)

If you want to survive for any length of time in the wilderness you have to be able to forage for food and water. Of the two, water is the most important because without water you will die and die quickly. Food is the secondary consideration.

You should have a minimum of 1 week's food in your B.O.B. Bag and 3 days of emergency rations in your G.O.T.H. Kit. What to do after those supplies run out or what to do to make those durable supplies last longer is the subject of this chapter.

These skills, like any other survival skill, are fairly simple but they are something you need to practice before you absolutely need them. Forget any squeamishness about blood or killing or you will die. Meat is a high energy food source and it is practically impossible to adequately feed yourself foraging only for plants year round. If nothing else, growing seasons prelude that. In a survival situation you will also learn to eat, consume, or make use of just about every part of an animal, even the internal organs of animals which have plenty of uses besides eating.

WATER ACQUISITION

Water is the essential ingredient a person needs to stay alive. In a survival situation access to potable were can and probably will mean the difference between life and death and depending on your geographic location a considerable amount of your effort will go into ensuring you have it. Water can be found everywhere on earth in varying degrees of plenty; from the desert of Death Valley to the tropical rainforest. But water, like candy comes in many forms, some good and some not so good. The good news is that you can almost always take filthy water and make it clean enough to drink given minimal gear.

The first requirement is to find water. If you are in a temperate or jungle area this should generally not be a problem as there will be streams, ponds, lakes, and if near a built up area you can obtain residual water from buildings. The story is different in semi-arid and arid zones where you might find some standing bodies of water such as stock ponds but most streams will be seasonal at best and rivers are far apart. All is not lost though as water can be obtained literally anywhere if you know how to go about it.

Once you have found some water you cannot just drink it, any water you drink must be purified first. In a perfect world your water would be treated to remove chemical and biological contaminants plus solids. A real survival situation is far from perfect though and you will often have to settle for treating biologicals and removing solids and will only be able to do rudimentary chemical contamination removal. However, most chemical contamination can be avoided by carefully selecting **where** you get your water.

Once you have clean water, what do you do with it? Purified water should be used for drinking, food preparation, and brushing your teeth. You do not have to purify water for general hygiene although it is advisable to treat such water for gross material contamination i.e. getting the mud out of it.

Always assume every drop of water you obtain from anything other than your own supplies or a working municipal water system is contaminated. The height of stupidity is to become sick or even die because you were too lazy treat water based on a faulty assumption.

CONTAMINANTS

Water contaminants are broadly separated into three categories, solids, biological and chemical. Solids are things like dirt, plant matter, and other gross contamination that can be easily filtered out of water. Biological contaminants are the various parasites, bacteria, viruses, and other disease vectors present in naturally occurring, untreated water. Most can be removed or rendered ineffective fairly easily, a few cannot.

Two common biologicals that are difficult to remove are *Cryptosporidium parvum* and *Giardia*, both are resistant to chemical decontaminants such as Iodine and chlorine. Prions (disease causing proteins) are not destroyed by boiling although there is some evidence that chemical decontaminants make them less virulent if they do not eliminate them altogether.

Chemical contamination is hard to detect without specialized testing kits but there are some ways to avoid it. The most common chemical contaminants in water include, pesticides, heavy metals, and industrial waste. The best way to avoid these are to avoid areas where such contaminants are likely used in large quantities such as industrial farms, factory zones, and power plants or downstream from such areas. Obtaining water from areas where chemical contaminants were unlikely to have been used is the best way to mitigate this risk as removing chemicals requires equipment that is bulky and generally requires a power source. Not something you can hump around in your B.O.B. Bag!

A final note is that poisonous water will not have fish, mosquitoes, algae, etc. living in it. Given a choice between water free of algae and one in which plants are visible to drink from, pick the water source with plants in it every time.

FINDING WATER

Finding water can be either the least or the greatest of your worries depending on the season of the year and where you are.

HOUSES

If you can get into them unobserved, abandoned houses are an excellent source of potable water even if municipal water is no longer running. There are several places to look for potable water. Always check the tap first, even if there is no electricity if there is still water in the tank then the system might be under enough pressure to let water run from the tap.

Hot water heaters: A standard hot water heater holds anywhere from 35-50 gallons of freshwater. However, before taking water from a water heater make sure there are no electricity or gas lines still connected to the tank. All hot heaters have a drain valve near the bottom.

If you find a private well system there is probably a pressure tank connected to the system that has water in it and if you find the well borehole you can improvise a bucket and get water straight from the well. Modern wells have small bores so you will probably have to use a bucket made out of a soup can.

RUNNING WATER

In most places in the continental US east of the Rockies you should be able to easily find running water such as streams or rivers. The most important thing to remember about obtaining water from these sources is to try and always get water upstream of possible contamination sources. Also strive to avoid getting water from obvious drainage ditches, especially in agricultural areas as modern farming introduces plenty of short term contaminants into surface water as runoff from plants being sprayed and fertilized.

STANDING WATER

Standing water such as lakes, ponds, stock tanks, and even puddles should provide you with drinking water. Most standing water has many more solid contaminants such as mud in it and also generally has a higher bacterial load as well. To eliminate solids you can simply let water stand for a time to let the contaminants settle to the bottom of the container or strain the water through cloth. Always strain such water before using any type of filter as the larger contaminants will make filters clog much faster reducing their usable life. Standing water should as a matter of principle be treated twice for biologicals. I prefer boiling followed by a chemical treatment.

GROUND WATER

Ground water is the most difficult to get. Ground water is from wells or if you are very lucky you will find a spring. Spring water is generally clean-to drink if you get it straight from the source but prudence says treat it for biologicals anyway. Well water should always be treated.

SOLAR STILL/DISTILLATION

The last ditch method of obtaining water is both more difficult and perhaps the most time consuming. It has the saving grace of also being the one that will get you water just about everywhere in the world except maybe Death Valley or the Empty Quarter of the Arabian Peninsula. This is the solar still and to build it you need three things, a sheet of plastic or waterproof fabric, a few rocks, and a container. A solar still takes advantage of the fact that the earth is 70% water and therefore almost all dirt has some water in it. It is a simple and effective method for getting that water out so that you can survive off of it. This method uses the same physical property that makes a glass of ice water sweat in the summer.

To maximize your chance of getting a useful amount of water pick the spot for your solar still carefully. The best places for building a solar still are in dry streambeds, boggy areas, or low lying ground. The damper the soil you find, the more water you can harvest. However, as stated above, just about all dirt has some water bound up in it that you can extract. When you build a solar still is also important as the longer the still is in the sun or the heat of the day the greater the heat differential between the air inside and outside the still and the greater water production will be.

Building a solar still is actually the height of simplicity. Once you find a good spot dig a hole as deep as you can get it, twice as deep as your container is high as a rule, and roughly 1/3 smaller than the smallest width of your plastic sheet. Once your hole is dug place your container in the bottom and spread the plastic out over the top of the hole with a little bit of slack in it. Use the stones to anchor the plastic around the hole and try to seal it so that as little air as possible can circulate under your plastic. Take the last stone and place it in the center of the plastic so that the lowest point is over your container. Now sit back and wait. As the air inside the still gets warm the water will sublimate out of the dirt and onto your plastic where it will roll down and drip into the container. **Any water you get by this method must also be treated.**

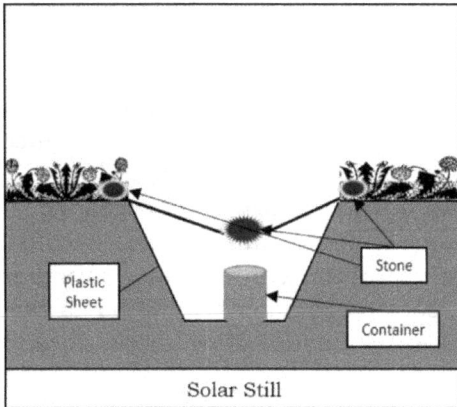

Plastic Sheet

Stone

Container

Solar Still

WATER PURIFICATION

The easiest way to ensure water is safe to drink and not contaminated by waterborne diseases is to boil it. However, boiling water is not 100% effective as boiling does not destroy disease causing prions.

If you are using a canteen or any other container with a lid to carry water do not forget to keep the lid area clean. It makes no sense to purify the water if it gets contaminated by your container when you drink out of it. If you use chemical purifiers such as chlorine or Iodine you can loosely cap the container and then pour a small amount of water out of the container and around the lid to disinfect it. You can pour a small amount of boiling water over the cap to achieve the same end.

BOILING

At Sea Level bring water to a rolling boil for a minimum of one minute to purify it for drinking. Prudence says you should let it boil for 4-5 minutes just to be sure. Boiled water will taste flat but flat is better than deadly. If you are at high elevations boil the water longer because water boils at a lower temperature with altitude. Another good thing is to have a pot or container with a lid to boil water in as this will reduce the amount of water you lose to steam.

BLEACH

Regular household bleach (Clorox™) is a great thing to purify water with as it takes very little bleach to purify a relatively large amount of water. Chlorine from a pool supply can be used as well but you must ensure that you know the chlorine concentration in any pool product you use as too much chlorine can be deadly. A chlorine concentration of 3-4 ppm is ideal for drinking water. A pool testing kit can be used to test the level of chorine in the water if you are unsure. If left to sit, chlorine will naturally dissipate to drinkable levels even if the water is super-chlorinated. The table on page 79 includes the number of drops of bleach to put into one liter of water to purify it for drinking. It takes more bleach to treat cold or cloudy water because cold an dirt affect the percentage of active chlorine in the water from reaching the levels required to effectively decontaminate the water.

Drops of Bleach to be added to 1 Liter of Water for purification		
Available Chlorine Concentration	Clear Water	Cold or Cloudy Water
1%	10	20
4-6%	2	4
7-10%	1	2
Read the label of the bleach container to determine the amount of available chlorine. Household bleach typically has 4-6% available Chorine.		
If you are unsure of the chlorine percentage use 10 drops and wait 30 mintues. If the water does not smell of chlorine then add 5 more drops and wait 10 mintues. Properly treated water should smell slightly of chlorine.		

IODINE

Iodine is also a very compact and effective method of water sterilization. Iodine water purification tablets can be purchased for minimal cost. A bottle generally contains 50 tablets good for roughly 6 gallons of water. Iodine can also be purchased as a 2% solution, which can also be used for water purification. The 2% solution is sold as a health supplement and also as Tincture of Iodine for wound disinfectant at pharmacies and drugstores.

When using a 2% Iodine solution use 5 drops for clear water and 10 drops for cold or cloudy water. Shake vigorously and let the water sit for at least ten minutes before drinking. If using tablets, follow the instructions on the bottle. Iodine treated water should have a slight chemical smell and taste to it.

When I was in the US Army we always saved our Kool-Aid pouches from MRE's to put in the canteens we had used to purify water in. This helped to make the water taste less disgusting. Iodine treated water tastes particularly nasty if you drink it without putting something in it.

PLANTS

Plants can and should be a valuable supplement to hunting for game, if not one of your primary means of acquiring food. The **most important** thing you can do is become knowledgeable about which wild plants in the area you expect to be in are edible. There are many poisonous plants that look similar to edible plants and if you eat the wrong one it can kill you.

I highly recommend staying away from eating mushrooms as there are hundreds of thousands of mushroom species and the vast majority of range from mildly poisonous to lick it and die poisonous. It takes an expert or much experience to reliably recognize which wild mushrooms are edible and which are not.

If you do find yourself in a survival situation and are unfamiliar with the local plant life you can use the Universal Edibility Test on the next page to determine if a plant is safe to eat. Use the test on all parts of the plant you plan on eating as some parts of the plant might be toxic while others are not.

It is beyond the scope of this book to include descriptions of the multitudes of edible plants that grow in the wild. A final word of caution, just because a plant looks like a common garden plant does not mean it is a wild cousin. Such plants can be deadly. For example, wild hemlock looks almost exactly the same as wild carrots but if you eat the greens from hemlock you will go the way of Socrates and die just like he did, by drifting off to the long dreamless sleep, whereas carrot greens just taste bad.

Universal Edibility Test

1	Test only one part of a potential plant at a time
2	Separate the plant into its basic components - leaves, stems, roots, buds, and flowers
3	Smell the food for strong or acidic odors. Remember, smell alone does not indicate if a plant is edible or not
4	Do not eat for eight (8) hours before starting the test
5	During the eight hours you abstain from eating test for contact by placing a piece of the plant part you are testing on the inside of your elbow or rest. Leaving it there for 15 mintues is usually enough time to allow for an allergic reaction
6	During the test period take nothing by mouth except for purified water and the plant part you are testing
7	Select a small portion of the plant part you are testing and prepare it the way you plan on preparing it to eat
8	Before placing the preparde plant part in your mouth touch a small portion to your outer lip to test for burning or itching
9	If after 3 mintues there is no reaction on your lip place the plant part on your tongue and hold it there for 15 mintues but **do not swallow it**
10	If there is no reaction throughly chew the plant part and hold it in your mouth for 15 mintues but **do not swallow it**
11	If no burning, itching, numbing, stinging, or swelling, or other irritation occurs during the 15 minutes, swallow the food
12	Wait eight (8) hours. If any ill effects occur during this period induce vomiting and drink a lot of water
13	If no ill effects occur eat approximatley 1/4 cup of the same plant part prepared the same way. Wait another eight (8) hours. If no ill effects occur the plant part **as prepared** is safe for eating

Caution

Test all parts of the plant for edibility as some plants have parts that both edible and inedible. Do not assume that a part that was edible when coked is edible raw. Test the part raw to assure edibility before eating it raw. The same part or plant may produce different reactions in different people.

HUNTING

Hunting is a pursuit that most people only do for sport. Survival hunting is entirely different than sport hunting as animals you would never take when sport hunting you will gladly eat when your survival is at stake. Examples are rats, skunks, raccoons, field mice opossums, and other small rodents which can be eaten as easily as deer and are much easier to catch. The trick with hunting is knowing where to find the animals as prey animals have evolved to be difficult to find.

If you have a firearm you can use it for hunting but remember that cartridges will probably be a finite resource in a survival situation and any bullet you put into a deer or rabbit you cannot use to defend yourself if necessary. Your best bet for a weapon to use for long term food procurement is to build a bow (see Chapter 4).

FINDING GAME

The key to finding game is being observant. Animals, like people, are creatures of habit. They tend to visit the same places to eat, drink, and sleep. If you are observant you will see the trails various animals make when moving from pace to place. These trails and watering/feeding sites are the places to hunt and trap because while animals are more alert while on the move or foraging you are also more likely to find them when they are on the move or at their watering or feeding sites. Once an animal reaches its rest spot they become very difficult to find. Trails are the best places to set snares and traps as generally multiple animals use the same trail which improves your chances of catching one of them. Bigger game such as deer are best hunted near their feeding areas.

Just as important as where to find animals is when to find them. You will generally not find much in the way of game in the middle of the day as most animals only really move around either at night or in the early morning and early evening spending most of the daylight hours resting and essentially hiding. Timing becomes important if you are hunting big game because believe me, a deer or rabbit can move through the woods at least ten times faster than you can.

Your first few weeks or days in a survival situation will probably be hungry as you get to know the movement and activity patterns of the animals in your area. Once you know these patterns and where to find animals the next thing to know is how to catch them so you can eat them.

SNARES/TRAPS

The easiest and most efficient way to hunt is to set snares. The downside is that while snares may keep you fed, they will probably not net you enough game to build up any sort of stock of preserved meat.

Snares are actually fairly easy to construct and set and much like trotlines they hunt themselves. There are two types of snares I will cover here; the spring snare and the deadfall trap.

SPRING SNARE

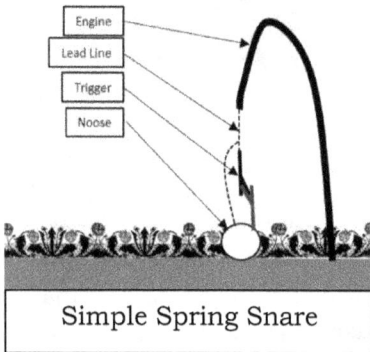

Engine
Lead Line
Trigger
Noose

Simple Spring Snare

A spring snare consists of four elements:

1. Noose – this is self-explanatory. I generally prefer to make snare nooses out of thin wire such as .014" piano wire. You can also strip the wire core out of electrical cords for this if you have to. Wire is preferred because it holds the shape of the noose better and does a better job of strangling the prey.

2. Trigger – this is a two-part item that consists of two lengths of wood fashioned such that they interlock and will stay in place under tension but will disengage when disturbed. Think of a

94

wooden version of the release on a mousetrap to get an idea of what I am talking about here. The trigger is fairly easy to whittle out of two short sticks.

3. Lead Line – the lead line is a length of cord or wire that goes from one side of the trigger to the engine and is also connected to the noose.

4. Engine – this is whatever device, most commonly a sapling, that you contrive to yank on the noose when the snare is triggered that both sets the snare and, if done correctly, delivers a killing snap to the neck of the prey. Killing the animal quickly is not just humane, it cuts down on the release of flight hormones in the animal and thus the meat will not taste as gamy when cooked.

DEADFALL TRAP

A deadfall trap is if anything, even simpler than a spring snare. It does not catch as much a spring snare though and these kind of traps sometimes don't kill the prey immediately often leaving a wounded animal time to get out of the trap and slink off to die somewhere leaving you with a sprung trap and no meal.

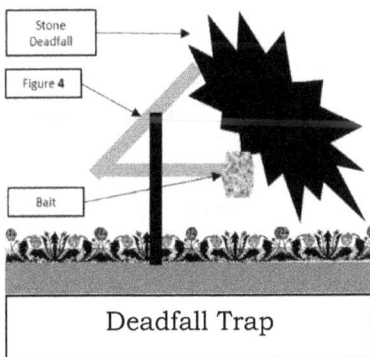

Stone Deadfall

Figure 4

Bait

Deadfall Trap

This kind of trap requires three sticks and the deadfall itself. The deadfall can be anything, a rock, a tree trunk, a box, etc. as long as it is big enough to trap or kill the intended target animal. To build this trap you take your three sticks and notch them such that they fit together into a figure **4**. The top diagonal of the **4** balances the deadfall while the cross bar of the **4** is under the deadfall and is baited. The sticks are arranged such that when an animal attempts to eat or take the bait they trip the deadfall and it falls on them trapping or killing them.

Both the spring snare and the deadfall take a little bit of practice to get right but they are quickly mastered and once mastered they can provide you with a steady source of meat, even in the winter months.

DRESSING GAME

Once you have killed an animal you have to prepare it for cooking.

BIRDS

After killing the bird, remove its feathers by either plucking or skinning. Skinning does remove some of the food value. Next open up the body cavity and remove the entrails, saving the craw (in seed-eating birds), heart, and liver then cut off the feet. Now your bird is ready to be cooked.

SKINNING AND BUTCHERING GAME ANIMALS

Always bleed game animals by cutting their throat. Bleeding them makes the meat last longer before spoiling. If possible, clean the carcass near a stream. Holding the carcass upside down, split the hide from throat to tail ensuring that you cut around the sexual organs. Remove the musk glands to avoid tainting the meat. For smaller mammals, cut the hide around the body and insert two fingers under the hide on both sides of the cut then pull both pieces off. When cutting the hide always turn the blade up after inserting it under the skin so that you only cut the

1 Cut the hide around the body.

2 Insert two fingers under the hide on both sides of the cut and pull both pieces off.

Field-dressing small game

hide. This will also help avoid getting animal hair on the meat. Animal hair is fiendishly difficult to get off the meat for some reason. Rabbits in particular have a depressing tendency to lose a lot of hair while being cleaned.

Remove the entrails from smaller game by splitting the body open and pulling the guts out with your fingers. Don't forget the chest cavity. For larger game (deer, hogs), cut the gullet away from the diaphragm and roll the entrails out of the body. Cut around the anus and then reach into the lower abdominal cavity to grasp the lower intestine and pull to remove it. Remove the bladder by pinching it off and cutting it off below your fingers. If you spill urine on the meat wash it immediately to avoid the meat being tainted and becoming inedible.

Save the heart and liver and cut them open inspecting them for signs of worms or other parasites. Inspect the liver's color as well as that can indicate a diseased animal. The liver should be deep red or purple in color with a smooth, wet surface. If the liver appears diseased, throw it away. However, a diseased liver does not necessarily indicate you can't eat the muscle tissue.

Alternatively you can gut a rabbit without using a knife at all by squeezing and flinging it. I learned how to do this as a kid. To do this you grasp the rabbit just below the ribs with both hands and start squeezing and working your hands towards the tail until the abdominal cavity feels very tight. Be careful not to squeeze too hard or the entrails will

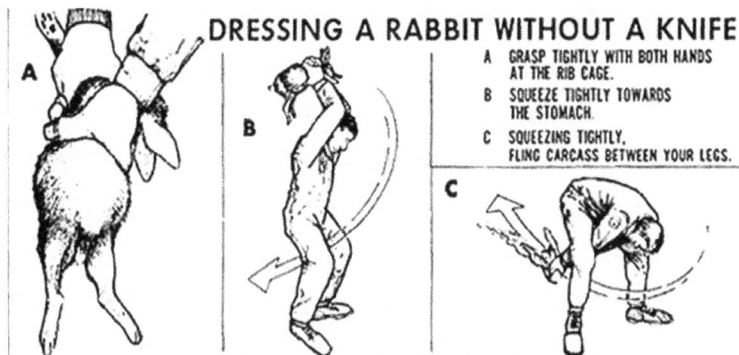

DRESSING A RABBIT WITHOUT A KNIFE

A GRASP TIGHTLY WITH BOTH HANDS AT THE RIB CAGE.

B SQUEEZE TIGHTLY TOWARDS THE STOMACH.

C SQUEEZING TIGHTLY, FLING CARCASS BETWEEN YOUR LEGS.

burst inside the rabbit and ruin the meat. Once the

abdomen is tight keeping ahold of the rabbit fling the body sharply. When you fling the rabbit if you do it right the entrails will come flying out of the anal opening and all you will have to do is finishing pulling the large intestine out. Make sure nobody is standing behind you or they will get a face full of rabbit guts.

With larger game it is extremely helpful and useful to hang the carcass by its back legs when possible. To help larger game hold longer before spoiling sever the jugular and let the blood drain overnight before butchering. It sounds disgusting but if the animal is healthy you can drink the blood which is very nutritional.

Cut along each leg from above the foot to the cut you made field dressing it then remove the hide by pulling it away from the carcass cutting the connective tissue where necessary. *If you need it you can save and cure the skin to make leather.* Cut off the head and feet and discard them.

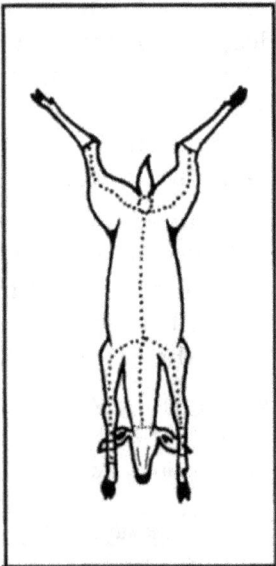

Lines for dressing large game

Cut larger game into manageable pieces. First, slice the muscle tissue connecting the front legs to the body. Since there are no bones or joints connecting the front legs to the body on four-legged animals this should be relatively easy. Cut the hindquarters off where they join the body. You have to cut around a large bone at the top of the leg and cut to the ball and socket hip joint. Cut the ligaments around the joint and bend it back to separate it, this sometimes takes quite a bit of force. Cut out the large muscles (the tenderloin) that lie on either side of the spine and separate the ribs from the backbone. There is less work and less wear on your knife if you break the ribs first and then cut through the breaks, a hatchet comes in handy for this. You can further prepare the carcass for cooking or preserving by cutting the meat into manageable pieces. The exact size and thickness of the pieces depends on what you are going to do with the meat.

COOKING

Cook large meat pieces over a spit or boil them. You can stew or boil smaller pieces, particularly those that remain attached to bone after the initial butchering, as soup or broth. You can cook body organs such as the heart, liver, pancreas, spleen, and kidneys using the same methods as for muscle meat. You can also cook and eat the brain or alternately use the brain in preparing the skin as leather. Cut the tongue out, skin it, boil it until tender, and eat it, the tongue is surprisingly tasty and almost pure muscle.

PRESERVING

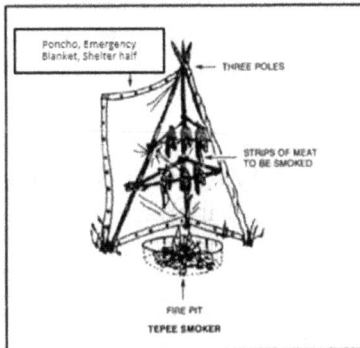

Poncho, Emergency Blanket, Shelter half

THREE POLES

STRIPS OF MEAT TO BE SMOKED

FIRE PIT
TEPEE SMOKER

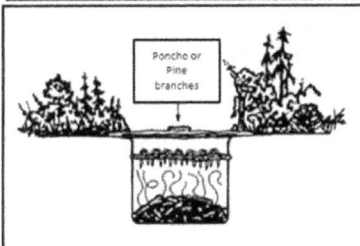

Poncho or Pine branches

Pit Smoker

Meat does not have to be cooked and eaten right away as there are several different methods you can use in the wilderness to preserve meat for later. My personal favorite method is to smoke it, mainly because this gives the meat some flavor.

SMOKING MEAT

To smoke meat, prepare an enclosure around a fire. Two ponchos snapped together will work but you can also build an enclosure out of tightly stacked pine branches or any other material that will not easily

99

melt. The fire should not be big or hot. The intent is to produce smoke, not heat. Do not use resinous wood such as Pine or Cypress in the fire because its smoke will ruin the meat. Use hardwoods such as oak, nut tree or fruit trees to produce good smoke. The wood should be somewhat green. If it is too dry to produce a lot of smoke, soak it in water for 12-24 hours. Cut the meat into thin slices, no more than two inches thick, rub some salt on the meat if you have any and drape the slices over a frame making sure none of the meat touches another piece.

Keep the poncho or branch enclosure around the meat to hold the smoke in and keep a close watch on the fire. Do not let the fire get too hot. Meat smoked overnight in this manner will last about 1 week. Two days of continuous smoking will preserve the meat for 2 to 4 weeks. Properly smoked meat will look like a dark, curled, brittle stick and you can eat it without further cooking. If you do not have a poncho or way to make a teepee you can also build a pit smoker out of readily available material in the forest. The disadvantage of a pit smoker is that you can only smoke small amounts of meat at a time in a pit because of size limitations.

DRYING MEAT

Meat can also be preserved by drying it. Prepare the meat by cutting it with the grain into 1/4 inch thick strips. Hang the strips of meat on a rack in full sunlight in an area with good air flow. Keep the strips out of the reach of animals and covered to keep flies and other insects off the meat. Allow the meat to dry completely before eating it. If the meat is properly dried it will have a dry, crispy texture and will not feel cool to the touch. If it does feel cool then it is not safe to eat.

FREEZING

In cold climates or during the winter you can freeze and keep meat indefinitely. Freezing is not a means of preparing it for consumption though as bacteria go dormant in the cold. You still have to cook it before eating to avoid becoming ill.

BRINE AND SALT

You can preserve meat by soaking it thoroughly in a saltwater solution for 24-48 hours. Prepare the solution by pouring salt into the water until it no longer dissolves but starts to collect on the bottom of your container. Ensure that the solution covers the meat completely.

You can also use salt by itself but salt curing meat takes a long time so this method is only suitable in a long term camp. To properly salt meat you trim off the parts of the cut that you will not later eat. Once the meat is trimmed wash it and pat it thoroughly dry. You can add some spices to the meat at this point to enhance the flavor when you eventually eat it. Finally, the salting. Rub salt thoroughly into the meat and then cover it **entirely** with a layer of salt. Covering the meat with salt eliminates bacteria and prevents future bacterial growth. Now hang the meat in a cool area. Cool means roughly 59°F so a cave or large sheltered underground root cellar is needed. The meat needs to hang and dry for roughly 3-4 weeks before it is properly cured. During the curing time check the meat at least every day taking especial care to smell it. If it smells like it is going bad it should be removed before it ruins the rest of your meat. To prepare your meat thoroughly wash off the salt before cooking it.

FISHING

If you find yourself in an area with running water or even decent sized ponds and streams fishing can be a lifesaver. With the right equipment and a little ingenuity fish are an easy way to supplement your diet. Indeed, some forms of fishing require no more effort than setting the line or trap and then coming back to check it later and remove four catch.

Fish provide an essential source of protein and also are chock full of vitamins. One thing you will find out is that as with animals, you can use just about everything from a fish to either eat or make something out of. Once caught fish should be prepared fairly quickly as the meat tends to go foul quite fast, especially in warm weather. Fish can be salted, dried, made into soup, fried, roasted, and cooked in an almost infinite variety of ways. Fishing, by whatever method however, generally requires patience.

TACKLE

A basic set of fishing tackle should be in both your B.O.B. bag and your G.O.T.H. kit. Fishing gear minus a rod is very compact and can fit into a container roughly the size of a deck of cards. At a minimum your fishing gear should include:

1. 100-200 feet of monofilament line (I recommend at least 8 pound test)
2. A dozen hooks
3. Two dozen split shot sinkers
4. A stringer or a length of cord to use as a stringer if you catch multiple fish to keep them alive until cleaning

This is the minimum amount of gear you need to get started. I would also pack at least 3-4 small cork bobbers. Plastic bobbers are too easy to break when you tote them around in a bag. If you have room I would concentrate on bringing hooks and line of several different weights. Sinkers and bobbers can always be improvised from woodland materials but hooks especially are difficult to fabricate from outdoor material and non-metal hooks are much more liable to breakage. There is a reason that hooks were one of the staple trade goods when Westerners started exploring the world in the 15th and 16th centuries. Next how to use the gear you have with you.

NOODLING/TICKLING

Noodling or Tickling is catching fish with your bare hands. It can be done and it doesn't take a lifelong woodsman to do it. It does take patience and quickness however. The easiest way to do this is in a fairly wide, clear stream that is no more than thigh deep, but preferably knee deep.

You have to determine a likely spot to find fish. During the day these spots are generally in areas sheltered from the main current such as behind rocks or in the lee of trees that have fallen into the water. These spots can be scouted from the bank. Simply look into likely areas and see if there are any fish there.

Once you have found a location frequented by fish wade into the water to your chosen spot and stand there. Bend at the waste and then wait. Fish are fairly stupid and if you remain still long enough they will come back. You wait until a fish decides you make good shelter and hovers in the current's lee by your leg and then grab it. I like to just toss the fish as far up the bank as I can when I grab it and then get out and kill it before it flops back into the water and leaves in an angry hurry.

Now that sounds simple, but is not that simple. Fish are fast and highly developed to notice and react to movement. If the fish is in your shadow as soon as you move it will be gone, if it is too deep when your hand breaks the water it will be gone. This is not the most efficient method of fishing but it does work after a fashion and with boatloads of patience.

SPEAR FISHING

Spear fishing is similar to noodling with the exception that you use a spear. The same basic rules apply as to finding a likely spot and patience.

Personally, I don't like to use a single pointed spear or spear fishing, I prefer to use a trident or frog gig when spear fishing. Fish are just too slippery to easily catch with a spear. Another thing is **don't** tie a knife to a stick and call it a spear for fishing, that is a good way to lose your knife. A better method is to cut a likely looking sapling that is at least eight foot tall and two inches in diameter. Use your knife to whittle one end down to a point and harden the point in your campfire or over a camp stove. Then if you lose your spear you are only out a few hours labor versus being out one of your most vital survival tools. Using the same method you can carve a trident out of a sapling if you pull or dig it up with the roots attached.

DROP LINE

This is what everyone thinks of when they think of fishing. A pole, a line, a hook, and a worm. You put the worm on the hook and the line in the water and start hauling them in. It is not quite that simple, but almost.

First, you do not need an expensive rod & reel to go fishing. A willow switch, line, hook, and worm are really all you need. The most important thing is that you tie the line to your pole securely and the hook to the line securely. Nothing is more irritating than watching your bobber swim away from a poorly tied line.

TROT LINE

A trotline is simply a length of rope stretched cross a body of water that has baited hooks on it at regular intervals. 550 Cord is an excellent cord to make a trotline with. I recommend a maximum trotline length of 75 feet to keep it from being too ungainly.

To make a trotline you must first determine how many hooks you want to put on the line. I always use an odd number, usually nine or eleven. Then measure out the length of line you need to cross the water with some slack for tying it off to an object on shore on both sides.

Starting in the middle of the line tie your first hook by tying a leader line to the trot line itself and then tying your hook to the leader such that when baited the hook will be at roughly the depth you want to fish. Using the center hook as a base start tying the rest of your hooks on the trotline. Tie one half of the remaining hooks on either side of the center hook leaving your last hook roughly 10-15 feet from the shoreline. Depending on how long your trotline is you will need to tie some floats on the trotline itself to keep the line from sinking once you set it. These floats will also help you tell if you have caught anything.

Once you have your trotline constructed it is time to bait and set it. First, bait all your hooks. You can bait your hooks with worms but I have found that grasshoppers or crickets make the best bait you can catch yourself. You can also use the guts of fish you have previously caught for bait. Set your trotline roughly one to two hours before sunset and leave it overnight. The next morning retrieve your line and depending on the season and frogginess of the fish you will have anywhere from one hook to a trotline full of fish caught while you were sleeping.

CLEANING

The flesh of practically all saltwater fish can be eaten raw. I think it tastes nasty but if you don't have a fire you can do it. However, fish taken close to shore should habitually be cooked as they commonly harbor harmful bacteria. By contrast, freshwater fish should always be cooked before eating as freshwater fish carry too many diseases that you can catch. Just to be on the safe side always cook any fish you catch.

There are different procedures for cleaning scaly and non-scaly fish. They are roughly similar but some important differences remain.

SCALY FISH

To clean a scaly fish, such as a Bass, Crappie, Perch, Trout, or Gar the first thing you need to do is remove the scales. To descale a fish you can use a de-scaling tool or a knife. With a knife you have to be careful not to cut the skin open as this damages the flesh. With practice this becomes easy.

To descale a fish start at the base of the tail and lightly scrape the cutting edge of your knife along the skin in the direction of the head. Keep descaling strokes short and be especially careful around the fins as descaling around the fins is not only difficult they can poke you and cause infection. Rinse the scales off your knife frequently with water, this makes the descaling a little bit easier.

Once you have all the scales loose rinse the fish with clean water to get all the scales off the fish. Scales are sticky and will get all over everything. Some people say descaling is unnecessary if you are going cook the fish whole. I say scales taste disgusting and can cut the inside of your mouth if you don't remove them so always descale a fish before you cook it whether you filet it or not.

NON-SCALY FISH

A non-scaly fish generally means a catfish. These fish are cleaned differently in that since they have no scales you should remove the skin before cooking them. To do this use your knife to carefully slice the skin on the underside of the fish from its anus to just before the gills, some people recommend cutting the skin along the top of the fish to start. Then cut the skin all the way around the body just behind the head and also just forward of the tail. Then carefully pull the skin off like an orange peel using the knife to loosen it when necessary. Be careful of the fins on Catfish as they sting and also have a poison in them that is very irritating. Lastly, rinse the fish with clean water.

GUTTING

Once you have a fish descaled or skinned the next step is to gut it. This is actually much simpler than you might think. Open the abdominal cavity by cutting into the fish near the anus and cutting forward to just behind the gills. Hold the knife so the blade side is out to avoid cutting open the entrails inside the fish. Once you have the abdomen open reach inside the fish and sweep the entrails out from back to front and throw them away or alternately keep them for use as bait. Then cut off the head unless it is a trout, which are normally cooked with the head on. Once you have the entrails removed rinse out the inside of the fish with clean water. Now you are ready to filet or cook the fish depending on your preference. I generally cook them whole and spice the hell out of them because I hate the taste of fish.

FILETING

If you want to filet and pan fry your fish you filet them in the following manner. Getting a good filet takes a very sharp knife and lots of practice. The essential method is to cut along the backbone from the head towards the tail with a gentle sawing motion to free the meatiest part of the fish from the spine and ribs. A proper filet has no bones in it at all. If you absolutely have to filet, start by fileting smaller fish and work your way up to larger fish as your technique improves.

COOKING

The simplest way to cook a fish in a survival situation is to impale a whole fish on a stick and cook it over an open fire. If you have a strong stomach boiling the fish with the skin on is the best way to get the most nutritional value. When you boil a fish save the juices for broth. Another method is to pack the whole fish into a ball of clay and bury it in the coals of a fire until the clay hardens. After it is done break open the clay ball to get to the cooked fish. Fish is fully cooked when the meat flakes off.

If you plan to keep the fish for later, smoke or fry it. To prepare fish for smoking, cut off the head and remove the backbone. If you have the salt available fish can also be salted but that tastes especially horrible and I do not recommend it.

CHAPTER 6 – COMBAT

"If you live among wolves you have to howl like a wolf."
Russian Proverb

This section is not designed to turn you or anyone else into Rambo or a member of SEAL Team Six, even if that would be pretty cool. It is designed to acquaint you with several different techniques for use if you find yourself in fight with someone determined to take what is yours. The techniques here should not be taken as gospel as they are always subject to adjustment based on local conditions.

Criminals and lowlifes will go for the low hanging fruit or "soft targets" as they are called by the military. Having a good working grasp of battlefield maneuver and defensive techniques makes you a hard target and thus less attractive to those that might mean you ill or just want your stuff.

If you have to fight remember the Cardinal Rule of combat is not to kill everything that moves, it is to achieve your objective, whatever that may be. Winning is something different. Eventually, in order to win, you might have to kill or wound opponents or demonstrate an ability to do so, to convince them to try for an easier target. Stubbornness and an unwillingness to quit are to a degree virtues in combat.

Let's face it, in a survival situation, or a *State of Nature* as the political theorists would have it, you want to make yourself as difficult a target as you possibly can. The basic rule is going to be do unto others before they do unto you. That does not mean you are going to kill everybody, or even most people you meet. It does however, mean that you will go into every encounter with someone you have never personally met before with a healthy dose of skepticism and a readiness to defend yourself and yours if necessary.

First off, if you have the notion that combat is simple, let me disabuse you of that idea real quick. Real life is not Hollywood and if you go haring off through a hail of gunfire as they do in movies you are likely to get killed. If that happens you won't have to worry about survival so you can go ahead and put this book down right now or give it to someone who is not a complete moron. Secondly, nobody that has job, a family, and a life is going to become a Navy SEAL or Delta Force trooper in their spare time even if they devote every free minute to trying. What you can do though is become competent enough at tactical maneuver that you are not simply a target but instead pose enough of a threat to any would-be aggressor to convince them to move along to that nice commune of dope smoking hippies in the next valley over.

Now that I have that off my chest and hopefully your full attention let's talk fieldcraft and combat skills for a second. There are two things about fieldcraft that you have to grasp almost immediately, I did not truly grasp them until my first firefight, which lasted about 20 minutes and left me feeling like I had just run a marathon with the

One, Fieldcraft seems deceptively simple and two, it is incredibly tiring and requires great stamina and endurance to keep it up for any length of time

world's fattest man on my back.

I will not go into any great tactical depth in this book but I will cover the basic techniques of fire and movement, how to cross a Danger Area, and field expedient defensive works. I will also cover weapons, both those to have beforehand and those you can improvise if you happen to live where weapons are prohibited or they are simply too expensive for you to purchase.

The difficulty in combat is not the complexity of the methods, it is the execution. It is extremely difficult to stay focused on the task at hand when you hear bullets snapping over your head. Bullets do in fact make a snapping sound, they don't whiz. Anybody who tells you they were not scared in combat is either crazy or a liar, probably both.

An aspect of military theory that applies to combat comes from United States Air Force COL John Boyd. Boyd wrote a seminal presentation in the 1970's called Patterns of Conflict in which he introduced the concept of the OODA Loop in combat operations. OODA is an acronym that stands for **Observation, Orientation, Decision, and**

Action. It describes what everybody does in combat. Boyd's breakthrough was that if you can get inside your opponent's OODA Loop then you can unhinge his actions and defeat him. His theory originally was developed in relation to air combat but has since been expanded to cover everything about military operations.

I am no more convinced of the OODA Loops relevance to operational and strategic principles than is Tom Kratman but I do think it applies to tactical situations. How it applies is that if you can get inside the decision cycle of your opponent and act faster than he can react to you then you can defeat him because is still trying to catch up with what you were doing 30 seconds ago instead of what you are doing now. When you are practicing, training, or actually in combat staying inside your opponent's OODA Loop is something to always strive to do as it increases your chances of winning.

There are a couple of things to mention before I start getting knee-deep that you should always keep in mind when doing anything that smacks of combat.

1. **Murphy's Law** –Moltke the Elder is the one who famously said that *"no plan survives first contact with the enemy"* although Clausewitz alludes to much the same phenomenon in his classic *On War*. It was true 150 years ago, it was true 2,000 years ago, and it is equally true today. As soon as something has to happen, it probably won't. The modern conception of this truism is called Murphy's Law, which reads: ***"If something can go wrong, IT WILL!"*** Always, and I mean always, keep that bastard Murphy in mind when you are planning anything. As sure as the Sun rises in the East, the moment you don't is when he will rear his ugly head and bite you in the ass.

2. (Operational Security) **OPSEC** – OPSEC is nothing more than ensuring that you keep your plans and preparations within your group and don't let anybody else know what you are doing.

For example, you don't want all the locusts/grasshoppers on your street knowing that you are prepared to take care of yourself if the worst ever happens because shortly after it does happen you won't be prepared anymore as they will have taken everything. This should be a no-brainer but is not because people generally like to brag and run their mouths.

3. **Noise/Light Discipline** – Means nothing more than staying as quiet as possible while out of contact and masking any light sources you use at night or even better, not using light during the hours of darkness at all unless you absolutely have to. You would be amazed at how far away you can see even the faintest light source at night with Night vision Devices (NVD's). I am talking kilometers here. In theory maintaining Noise/Light Discipline would seem to be deceptively easy. **It is not**. This is something you must constantly keep in mind. Sometimes just practicing this can save your life.

4. **Flexibility** – Don't let anything you read in this section be taken as dogma that must be followed or disaster will ensue. The Cardinal rule of combat is that it is never the same twice. Always adjust your operational methods to the situation in which you find yourself. You will react and operate differently in urban areas, dense forest, light forest, or plains. Use your head and think about things before you do them. There are very few combat tasks that are amenable to drilling despite the US Army's love of battle drills.

5. **Battle Drills** – I will make no bones about the fact that I am not a huge fan of battle drills. I think that there at most two situations where a Battle Drill is appropriate, everything else is situation dependent and over-reliance on Battle Drills where they don't really apply gets people dead. Why? Because by its very nature combat

is chaotic and unpredictable. Battle drills are just that, **drills**. They teach people to react a certain way to certain stimuli without regard to the actual situation. At times, this is the right thing to do, the vast majority of the time, it is not. I will cover the two dismounted Battle Drills I find appropriate later in this chapter.

6. **Recognition Signals** – Any group that you are a part of needs recognition signals, both far and near. These signals need to be agreed upon by all members of the party before you go anywhere. The far signal should include a distress signal. If your party has radios then far recognition can be done over the radio, if you do not then it should be done visually in whatever manner is agreed upon. Near recognition signals are nothing but a challenge and password. Passwords and other signals should be changed frequently. Just like with computer passwords you should try very hard to avoid repetition in the signals and passwords you choose.

7. **Quiet** – Something you see a lot of in movies that always cracks me up is everybody trying their hardest to be quiet in the middle of a firefight. **Forget that!** Once you are in a shooting fight it really doesn't matter how much you yell and staying quiet actually just contributes to your own party's confusion. Once you are in contact go ahead and yell and scream instructions and information back and forth, the enemy already knows you are there after all.

If you have the opportunity to attend a school for civilians that teaches combat techniques do so. Then **practice, practice, practice**. I personally like to go out and play paintball, which is not only fun but outstanding tactical training or you can make it so if you want.

Lastly, any type of combat techniques are best done in at least pairs. I don't care how high speed you are, if you go into a combat situation outnumbered 2, 5, or 10-1 you will probably die, get wounded, or be captured. Rambo would have died at least ten times in the first movie if he even managed to make it out of the police station in the first place. Therefore, it is best if you have at least one person you **implicitly** trust who you can bug out with. I am thinking wife or old combat buddy here. All the techniques I talk about take at least two people to do correctly and can easily be scaled up if there are more people in your party. I recommend a minimum party size of four people as the best compromise to maximize security and stealth.

TACTICAL MOVEMENT/DEFENSE

Tactical Movement and the Defense are three parts knowledge and one part ability in my book. Contrary to popular belief, it takes intelligence to be successful in combat. The days when any idiot off the block had the makings of a good soldier are long over.

It would be prudent to not only have this book but to acquire and study many of the manuals available on tactical movement and the defense long before you have to use them. Along with the typical military manuals you will find on any prepper's bookshelf I also recommend that you get ahold of some books on pre-modern combat and defense. There are several excellent works out there on castle/fortification construction and also a few on pre-modern firearm combat. Let's face it, if the worst happens most of the high-speed, low-drag assault rifles and pistols will be so much dead weight long before ammo runs out because of a lack of spare parts. Spare parts for modern weapons require precision machinery and skills that not many people possess. However, Black Powder is fairly easy to make and so are the weapons that use it.

That being said, reading something out of a book and putting it into practice are two different things entirely. You must practice the combat techniques you will use before you have to actually put them into practice. The first time to use these techniques is not when someone is shooting at you. Practice creates both muscle memory of the movements you will use and familiarity so you know you can actually take a dive at a full run without crippling yourself. A final note is that not only are these techniques useful, they are somewhat fun and a great workout.

MOVEMENT FORMATIONS

Movement Formations are used by fire team to facilitate reaction and control depending the circumstances and terrain. There are essentially six formations Line, Vee, Echelon (left & right), Diamond, Wedge, and File. The leader of the group is indicated by the **TL** circle. These positions give the leader the best ability to see and control the entire group. Except for the file, most of these formations are only adopted when you are actually in a fight or expect one to start shortly.

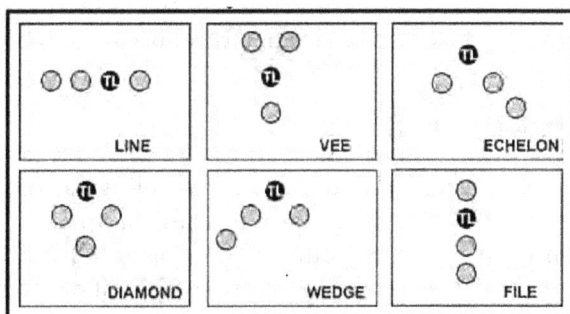

METHODS OF MOVEMENT

There are three methods of movement and they apply whether you are in a vehicle or walking. I will briefly describe the three.

- Traveling
- Traveling overwatch
- Bounding overwatch

Because I am partial to the idea of a minimum group of four all my diagrams show four members in the group. Larger groups just scale up from the core size of four. In the military the four positions in a column all have names. The man in front is the Point Man, second place is Slack, third

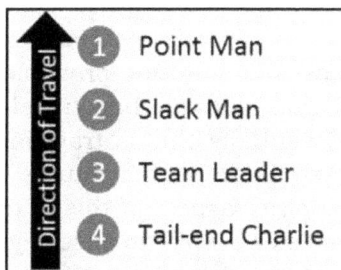

1 Point Man

2 Slack Man

3 Team Leader

4 Tail-end Charlie

Direction of Travel

is the Team Leader, and fourth in the rear is Tail-end Charlie. Each man has different responsibilities while on the move and at the halt.

A clock method is used when moving and 12 o'clock is always the direction of travel. Any other system is too difficult for everyone to keep up with. Sometimes simplest is the best. All party members watch the same sector whether on the move or at the halt. The point obviously keeps an eye out to the front while the Slack man looks to the left, the Team Leader to the Right and Tail-end periodically looks backwards while on the move and continuously watches the rear at the halt. Those are the general areas of orientation. Now on to actual movement methods.

TRAVELING

Old vets, and new, call Traveling be-bopping down the street although it is not that simple. To use the traveling technique your group essentially travels in a straight line without stopping with the different members of your party watching their different sectors for threats or dangers. Use this method only when you don't expect anything bad to happen, which after the crash means probably never. This is simply where all elements move at the same rate of speed. It is the fastest but least secure method of moving in a potentially hostile area. Intervals between people are roughly 10-15 feet depending on the thickness of vegetation and lines of sight.

TRAVELING OVERWATCH

Traveling Overwatch is used when contact is possible but not probable. This movement technique is slightly slower than traveling but offers increased security. Essentially this is traveling with increased distance (20-25 feet) between individuals and the formation is staggered. Another aspect of this is that the trail man falls back every once in a while to ensure you are not being tailed. Traveling overwatch is a compromise between speed and security.

BOUNDING OVERWATCH

Bounding overwatch is used when you expect to get into a fight in the near future. Bounding means just what it says. Essentially half the group moves forward while the other half stays put and provides security and overwatch. Once the first group is set the second group moves up to and then past the first group to another position while the first group provides security. The groups alternate moving like this until you get where you are going or you get into a fight. This is the slowest but most secure method of movement.

COVER VS. CONCEALMENT

I have to discuss these two items and the difference between them as they are critically important if you are to survive your first firefight. Cover and concealment are not the same thing although many people think they are. The essential difference is *cover will stop you from getting shot and concealment stops you from being seen.* Objects on the battlefield can be one or the other or both depending on the object.

An example of **cover** that is not concealment is an armored vehicle. If you are in an armored vehicle you are generally immune to small-arms fire, thus you have cover, but since armored vehicles tend to be large and easily spotted you would not have concealment.

An example of **concealment** is a bush. You can hide behind a bush and not be seen but a bullet marked *To Whom It May Concern* can go right through the bush and still kill your ass. Thus you have concealment but not cover.

An example of both **cover and concealment** is a two person camouflaged fighting position below the military crest of a hill. Because it is camouflaged the enemy may know there are fighting positions on the hill but they cannot pinpoint them thus you are concealed. Further, because you are squared away and dug your hole armpit deep with grenade sumps and 18 inches of overhead cover a random bullet or even an aimed one will probably be stopped so you also have cover.

It is extremely critical that you keep this in mind if you ever find yourself shooting at someone and being shot at in return. Hopefully, the guy shooting at you has no experience or knowledge and is stupid enough to think concealment is as good as cover. Which notion you will quickly disabuse him of as you demonstrate to him that they are not because you have paid attention and understand the difference.

TACTICAL FIRE AND MOVEMENT

Fire and movement is what you do once the shooting starts. Like any other combat task it is simple in concept but difficult in execution. The idea is that one person fires at the opponent to keep their heads down while the other moves in the desired direction of movement. It is easier to do this in the assault but it can also be done as you are retreating. Actually, the hardest combat task to do is retreat because not only are you going the wrong way, once the enemy sees you leaving he gets bolder and redoubles efforts to kill you.

There are actually three ways to move while in contact:

- **3-5 second Rush**
- **High Crawl**
- **Low Crawl**

Which method you choose depends upon the situation.

3-5 SECOND RUSH

This is exactly what it sounds like. You get up from your covered and concealed position and haul-ass as fast as you can for 3-5 seconds to your next covered and concealed position. Hopefully you have a teammate who will provide covering fire while you do this. Otherwise you are just a fast target for 3-5 seconds for whoever is shooting at you.

HIGH CRAWL

You have probably seen this move in the movies many times and thought it was the low crawl, it aint. The high crawl is lighting fast compared to the low crawl. Essentially the high crawl is used whenever fire is too heavy to rush or concealment is good enough that you can move unseen with this technique.

To high crawl you simply cradle your rifle and crawl forward on hands and knees keeping your body as low as possible. Your torso should be no more than 2-3 inches off the ground as you high crawl. Take particular care to keep

The High Crawl

your rear-end from sticking up too high as I am told that getting shot in the ass is painful if not generally life threatening. Plus, waving your ass around is a good way to attract lots of unwanted lead in your direction.

LOW CRAWL

I don't think the low crawl has been in too many movies, probably because it sucks so much to do it and

The Low Crawl

when done right it is downright painful. The low crawl is what you do to cross an area that is in plain view of the enemy and you want to be as little exposed as possible. In all honesty, if I had an area I had to low crawl across and I knew the enemy was there, I would find a different way to get where I was going if at all possible. Sometimes it is not possible and as a result we have the low crawl.

To perform the low crawl you loop your rifle over your dominant arm (right in my case), get as close to the dirt as you can and then start moving. You do this by simultaneously sliding your non-dominant arm forward, grabbing dirt, and sliding your dominant leg up flat along the ground and then pushing yourself forward along the ground. I mean literally sliding along the ground trying to become one with it. If we could come up with a little bulldozer blade for a helmet that would be ideal. Low crawling for any distance is extremely tiring. Tiring, as in low-crawling for 100m makes you want to drink a beer and spend the rest if the day on the couch, just absolutely exhausting. If you low crawl any distance and are not just bone tired then you are not doing it right. The low craw is an absolute last resort movement method because if you have to low crawl then you are probably in a world of hurt already.

BATTLE DRILLS

As stated above, I am not a big believer in Battle Drills. They can teach you the right reactions for some situations but the wrong reactions for others. Contrary to popular belief there are very few situations in combat where you have zero time to think about your next move, often you have 1-5 seconds and believe me, 1 second can seem like an eternity in combat.

I recommend being intimately familiar with only two **dismounted** battle drills for the amateur, actually anybody, to learn and practice. They are extremely simple and when you are caught in their specific situations they are the right move every time. They are not guaranteed to save your life because there are no guarantees when someone is shooting at you. They are:

1. React to near contact
2. React to far contact

I am willing to go along with these two drills because following them is the correct thing to do 99% of the time or more. These drills instill actions that if executed promptly increase your personal chance of survival and that of those in your party. That being said, if you are the point man expect that you will probably die if you are ambushed. Be prepared for it and don't let it stop you from doing what has to be done. Being point while dismounted is no different than being the #1 guy going into a house on a raid. The pucker factor is unreal and the release when you walk away is one of best feelings you will ever have in your life. Think of your relief after a near-miss car accident and multiply that by a million. Enough about that, on to the drills themselves.

React to Near Contact – Imagine yourself, _and your family_ after the world ends, tooling down a trail on the way to wherever you're going when suddenly several rifles or guns start firing at you from about 10 feet to your right. **What do you do if you are not cut down in the initial burst?** What most people would do, including many soldiers, is freeze, shit their pants, then curl up on the ground and whimper while they wait to die. That is the absolute wrong thing to do for multiple reasons the most important of which is the dying part.

What you do (since you are confident and well-practiced) is turn into the source of the fire, let out a BraveHeart worthy blood-curdling yell and charge straight into the fire while shooting back and being intent on killing whichever sorry bastard had the gall to shoot at you. That is **Reacting to Near Contact.**

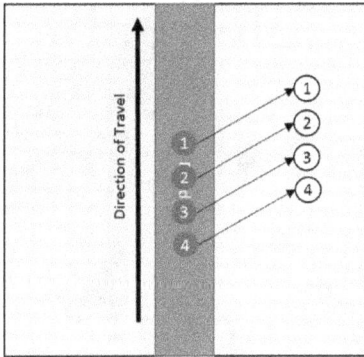

The **React to Near Contact** battle drill is for when you are dismounted (walking) and the people shooting at you are within 50 feet. If they are any farther away they have plenty of time to get off a third, fourth, or even fifth shot before you can get close to them. Inside that distance and you running at them screaming bloody murder is liable to break their concentration enough to allow you to get close enough to kill them.

React to Near Contact

React to Far Contact – Reacting to Far Contact is a little different and it only works with a party of a minimum size of two although bigger **is** better in this situation. Far contact is anybody attacking you at a distance of from 50 to 300 feet away from you. Close enough that you might be able to do something effective yet far enough that it will take you some time to get to close grips with them.

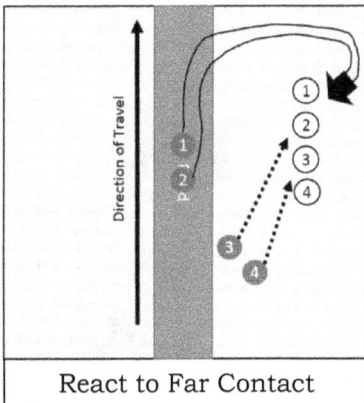

The way to deal with this is that everybody in your

React to Far Contact

125

party seeks immediate cover (notice I said cover not concealment). After everybody is down, the half of the party nearest those shooting at you starts laying down suppressive fire while the half furthest away maneuvers to take the ambushers in the flank. Which half maneuvers depends on where the ambush is at relative to your party and their disposition once everybody has gone to ground. This is where leadership comes in, somebody has to decide who will move and who will stay put.

CROSSING AND CLEARING DANGER AREAS

The easiest way to deal with a Danger Area is to avoid it by going around or picking a different route. That is not always possible so there are several methods to get across one. Keep in mind that crossing a Danger Area always involves risk, a risk that you must determine is acceptable given the urgency or requirement to get to the

Let's define a *Danger Area*: A *Danger Area* is any feature, terrain or man-made, upon which you would be exposed to unfriendly observation and possible fire while traversing said feature. Examples include roads, clearings, parking lots, ridgelines, streams, rivers, and other water features.

other side in an expeditious manner.

I will discuss three methods of crossing a Danger Area in order of their speed of execution. All these clearance methods require at least two people but work best if you have a group of four or more people in your party for maximum security. All my example illustrations will show four people and how to cross a road, crossing any other Danger Area is just a variation on the theme. Keep in mind that nothing about these methods is set in stone and you must adjust your operational methods to the situation you find yourself in. Flexibility is a lifesaver in combat situations.

1. Scroll the Road – used to cross linear Danger Areas
2. The Cloverleaf

A good practice when using the Cloverleaf or Box Method is to always have the two trail people in your party clear the far side. That way once the entire party is across and you start to move the trail team that pulled security on the far side can just fall in at the end of your column after the rest of the party has passed them.

3. Box Method

Scrolling the Road is used when you have to cross a danger area fast because your speed of movement is important. This could be because you need to get somewhere or because you are moving away from contact. It is very simple, very quick, and very dangerous. This method should only be used if you are really in a hurry because there is a risk that your element can be split if you come into contact while executing it.

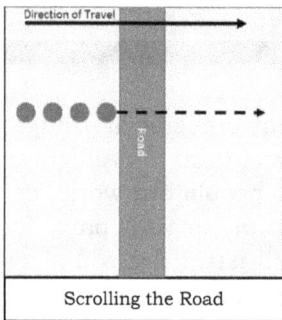
Scrolling the Road

To **Scroll a Road** your group simply briefly pauses at the Danger Area, quickly scans for threats and if none are seen then the first person crosses the Danger Area (hauling ass) and then continues to move, as soon as the first person is across the next person goes, and this continues until the entire party is across the Danger Area.

The Cloverleaf is the next method of crossing a Danger Area. It is a variation of the **Box Method** and is slightly more secure than just scrolling across a road but less secure than the **Box Method**, which while the most secure, is also the most time consuming.

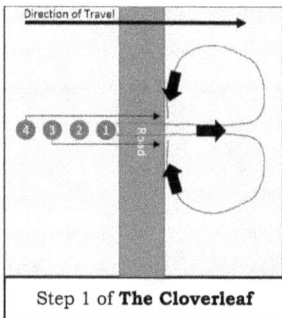
Step 1 of **The Cloverleaf**

Use the **Cloverleaf Method** when you are in kind of a hurry but not in so much of a hurry that you can't afford a few minutes to at least ensure a modicum of security.

When you approach a Danger Area and decide on the **Cloverleaf Method** the entire party will stop on the near side of the Danger Area and then one person will go across and secure the far side. As soon as the person on the far side is across a second person will cross and join them while the rest of the party remains on the near side of the Danger Area.

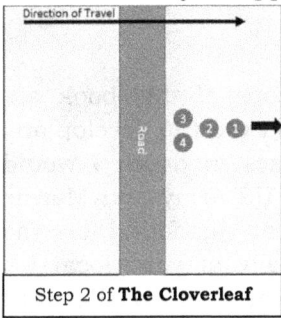

Step 2 of **The Cloverleaf**

The #1 and #2 people will then do a semi-circle in opposite directions to a depth of at least 25m depending on the size of your party looking for signs and evidence of unfriendly presence and complete their semi-circle at the point where they started. If the area is secure both people stay at the crossing point. One person pulls security in the direction of travel while the other communicates with those in the group that have not yet crossed. Once far side security is set let the party members on the near side know using your recognition signal. The near side people then come across one at a time. As the near side people come across a perimeter is formed and once all the party is across you continue to move.

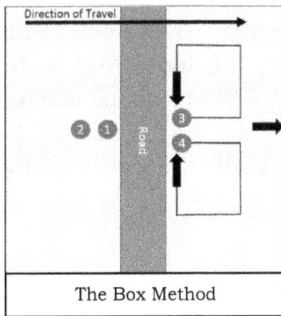

The Box Method

The **Box Method** is the most secure way to cross a danger area, but also the slowest. It is essentially the same as the **Cloverleaf Method** with the exception that you push people out to the flanks on the far side of the danger area before you bring your party across. This is also the most manpower intensive method as it actually requires a minimum party size of 5 people to do it right.

DEFENSIVE WORKS

Mostly what is within the scope of this book are foxholes and hasty fortifications. If you want to develop any kind of long-term defenses or defenses in depth I would recommend you consult the relevant US Army and Marine Combat Engineer Manuals, which can be found on the internet, purchased online, or generally at your local US Army Surplus store. The three to really get are FM 5-13 Engineer Field Handbook (the 1964 Version), FM 5-15 Field Fortifications (the 1944 Version), and FM 5-34 Engineer Field Data (the newest –currently 2005).

Something to also keep in mind is perhaps resurrecting some ideas from the Middle Ages and there are several books written by academics about medieval fortifications that are of interest and present some ideas that have gone out of fashion. Of particular interest should be the timber Motte and Bailey castles of the period of the Norman Conquest in England and 7th – 10th Century Eastern European timber Ring-Forts. A caveat when looking at medieval fortifications is that unless you are thinking about building something along the lines of the *Trace Italienne* all medieval style fortifications will need to be fronted and backstopped with plenty of loose earth to absorb both explosives and rifle fire. There is a reason nobody builds castles anymore, and that reason is gunpowder as stone or timber Curtain Walls are pathetically easy to breach with explosives.

FIGHTING POSITIONS

I will describe two hasty foxholes and a couple of obstacles. Anything else is, as previously stated, outside the scope of this book.

If you don't have a folding shovel or military style entrenching tool (e-tool) in your Bug-Out Bag you are wrong! There are many uses for an e-tool but the one it was designed for is digging a hole to save your butt in a bad situation. If you ever do any reading of memoirs from the World Wars, Korea, or even the Civil War Petersburg Campaign you will read many accounts of soldiers digging, digging all the time, pretty much digging every time they got the chance. Digging deep saved lives in many instances. The same will be true of you if you have to stay in one place for any length of time because of weather, injury to a party member, or illness.

The smart word about static positions in the US Army, and I hated it, is to continually improve your position. What starts out as a two inch deep scrape will almost have a living room and bedroom by day three. Something to always remember is to **never** take camouflage from in front of your position. Nothing gives a position away as much as some hacked off branches or holes where you dug plants up to camouflage your position. **Always take camouflage from the rear of your position but not near enough for an opponent to see it.** Also, if you are going to be somewhere for any length of time try and use whole plants, not only do they look more natural they save you the effort of cutting fresh camouflage every morning, which gets real old and will also denude your surroundings amazingly fast.

There are two kinds of foxholes. One is a slit trench and is what we called titty deep in the Army, it is about 18 inches deep and long enough for you to lay down in. Its purpose is no more than to get you below ground level and below most of the flying metal that is coming your way. The second is a full-up foxhole with overhead cover, firing ports and grenade sumps. The first takes about twenty minutes to dig, the second anywhere from 3-8 hours depending on the ground you are trying to dig through.

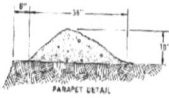

PARAPET DETAIL

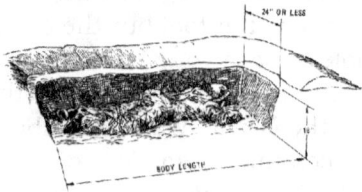

24" OR LESS

BODY LENGTH

Slit Trench

A complete two-man foxhole is a hole about 24 inches wide by 4 feet long by between 5-6 feet deep. The rule of thumb for depth is armpit deep on the shortest guy in the hole. It should have a grenade sump at either end to kick grenades, homemade or otherwise, into so they don't kill you and a minimum of 18 inches of overhead cover. The overhead cover should be timber and earth construction. Not only does this help deal with concussion the combination of timber and earth stops bullets better than either will alone.

A more complete illustration of the sequence is on the next page.

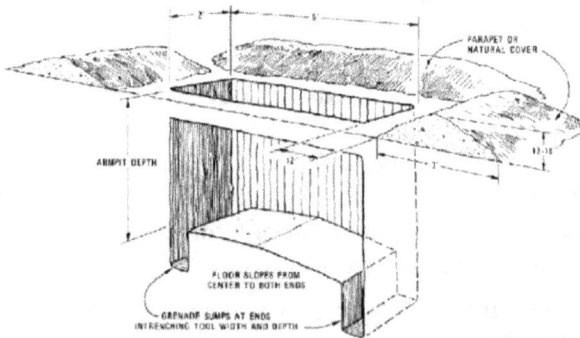

PARAPET OR NATURAL COVER

ARMPIT DEPTH

FLOOR SLOPES FROM CENTER TO BOTH ENDS

GRENADE SUMPS AT ENDS INTRENCHING TOOL WIDTH AND DEPTH

The two-man foxhole/fighting position

FRONT SUPPORT

The front supports are high enough so men can shoot from beneath the overhead cover when it is completed.

REAR SUPPORT

CONSTRUCTING ROOF

The roof is made of logs 4"–6" in diameter placed side by side across the supports.

WATERPROOFING

A water-repellant layer, such as waterproof packing material, plastic membrane, or a poncho, is then laid over the logs.

CAMOUFLAGE OVERHEAD COVER

18"–20" of dirt is added and molded to blend with the slope of the terrain.

OBSTACLES

First off, there are two very important things to remember about obstacles. One, they will not stop a determined enemy, and two, they are useless if not monitored. That being said, obstacles can prove useful to slow an enemy down, whittle away the amount of combat power a hostile group or force can bring to bear, and perhaps most importantly, get them to go where you want them to go.

I will separate the obstacles into two kinds, Early Warning and Mobility.

EARLY WARNING OBSTACLES

Basically an early warning obstacle is not actually an obstacle at all, it is simply something that when disturbed or tripped by an enemy makes a noise or light signature that alerts you that something is there, even if you don't know exactly what it is.

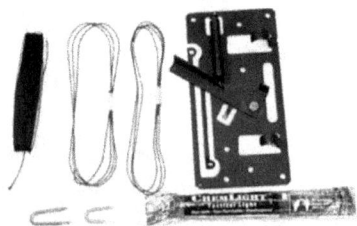

Chem-light Trip Flare

These have been used historically going back to at least Roman times that I am aware of. In the modern era the military uses trip flares, which are not available commercially and trip chemlights, which are. These devices both work on the same principle in that somebody hits a trip wire which activates a spring loaded igniter or a bar that breaks the chemlight. The chemlight devices are even cooler because if you have night-vision devices you can use infrared chemlights that are only visible in night-vision gear and make no visible light. The best thing about the chemlight trip flare is that as long as you have chemlights, you can re-use them. The chemlight flares are relatively cheap as well selling in the neighborhood of $20 for the flare assembly with replacement chemlights running about $20 per box of ten.

That is a high-tech solution. There are plenty of low-tech solutions as well. Many of these can be quickly set up and require nothing more than some ingenuity and some 550 cord, which if you are squared away you have in both your **G.O.T.H.** and **B.O.B.** bags. 550 Cord has so many uses it is almost as necessary as water.

The easiest early warning device you can set up is simply scatter some dry twigs in a circle around your campsite. Set them far enough away that even if someone were running you would have time to reach for a weapon before they got to you. I recommend that you place them in a circle 25-35 feet away from where you will be sleeping. One of the best things about this method is if you are in a wooded area you don't even have to camouflage them as the woods are full of branches and twigs lying around on the ground. You don't even have to do a full circle if you pick your campsite wisely, then you only have to put them on likely approach paths.

Another simple early warning device that takes some time and a little bit more equipment is a rattle device. To build this you need an empty metal can, some 550 Cord or wire, and some gravel. Any kind of metal can will work although I prefer aluminum soda cans as they are light, the uneven bottom makes a more effective rattle, and the pop-top has a ready-made handle hole for you to tie into.

All you need to do is put 3-4 pieces of gravel, no more or they won't rattle, into the can. Then find an appropriate spot on the approach path your can is supposed to guard. The best location is one with something to anchor your line to on both sides although forked sticks or tent pegs can be driven into the ground in a pinch. If you use sticks or tent pegs your device will not be as sensitive.

Tie the fixed end off to the anchor, it can be a rock, a tree stump, a low branch. Tie the other end of the line to your can leaving about 18 inches of slack beyond the second anchor. If this is hasty and not a long term device simply drape the loose line over the second anchor letting the weight of the can pull the line tight.

If you are using wire attach to the first anchor the same way. The difference is instead of tying off to the can run the wire through the pop-top and then stretch the wire taut anchoring it to the second anchor point.

You are all done. One homemade perimeter warning device. If anybody trips the line in the night they will knock the can around causing the gravel inside to rattle and letting you know there is an intruder. One hint: I like to put the line no lower than about knee height on an adult so that small critters (raccoons, possums, etc.) don't trip the line and wake me up for nothing. You can also achieve the same effect using bells like the ones you put on presents at Christmastime.

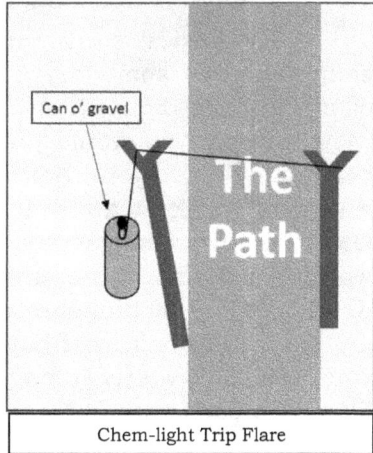

Chem-light Trip Flare

In effect the only limit on the type devices you can use is your imagination. I have seen references to using the speakers from greeting cards that play annoying music. My son also used to have an alarm that he got in a spy toy-set, which made use of an IR beam. Something similar could also be used, at least as long as the batteries held up.

MOBILITY OBSTACLES

A mobility obstacle is any obstace you put in place to either slow an opponent down or force him to go where you want him to go. The limitation on these types of obstacles is also your imagination. These can be just about anything from caltrops, induced landslides, wire, trees, or anything else. As stated, imagination is the best thing here, just get creative and see what you can come up with. In a survival situation one thing you want to think about is ensuring that you always have an exit from your obstaced enclave. Obstacles don't actually stop anybody, they only slow them down so unless you are ready to go out in a blaze of glory have an exit plan prepared and ready. In fact, it should be one of the first things you do and should be part of your planning.

Most mobility obstacles take considerable time and/or manpower to emplace and are only suitable if you are going to be somewhere for a while. I will only cover three here although there are many more to be found in FM 90-7 Combined Arms Obstacle Integration. These three are an Abatis, a Wall, and a Ditch, yes a ditch.

An Abatis is made using trees felled in a crisscross pattern such that they impede movement along a road or trail. The military plans on using explosives to drop trees and you can too if you know what you are doing and have explosives available but this obstacle can also be made by cutting the trees down with an axe or chainsaw. It should go without saying that the size of the tree to be felled is dependent on the type of traffic you want to stop. An Abatis can stop tanks if the trees are big enough but they have to be pretty big trees. For the purposes of this book we don't need to stop tanks only cars or people walking. The tree diameter to stop cars or wheeled vehicles is roughly 8-10 inches and to block a walking trail figure on using trees with a diameter of no less than 4-6 inches.

You start building an abatis on the side towards the opponent. The trees are cut such that they fall across the road or trail at an angle and make vees. The apex of the vees should point toward the opponent. Additionally, you should cut the trees on opposite sides in a back and forth "Z" pattern. You cut the first tree then cut the tree opposite it then return to the first side and cut the next one and so on. This way of cutting the trees ensures that they fall and interlock tangling together. Doing this ensures that somebody with a plow cannot simply push through the Abatis nor can they tie off a chain and quickly pull it apart.

A Completed Abatis

Next, the lowly ditch. You would be surprised at how effective a simple ditch can be if dug in the right spot with the proper orientation. The Roman Legions dug a ditch every day when they pitched camp. In fact, the Romans built an entire fort every day with streets, a wall, a ditch, and towers. Such effort is beyond the scope of this book.

If you dig a small two to three foot deep by four foot wide ditch at the base of your wall you not only increase the effective height of your wall, you also force any opponent to navigate an obstacle that will break his stride and slow him down before he hits your wall. If you are lucky he is stupid and breaks his leg too meaning you can probably go and kill him at your leisure. If you get really creative you can add fire-sharpened wooden stakes to your ditch and other traps and devices. If you have a claymore mine or two emplacing them to fire along the length of your ditch is an excellent idea.

To make a ditch the most effective you should camouflage it. This can easily be done by laying a grid of sticks across it and scattering the top of the grid with leaves and soil so that it matches the surround ground.

Last, a wall. The wall complements a ditch and can even be constructed of the spoil you take out of the ditch. You don't necessarily need an earthen wall though and it might even be counter-productive to build one for fear that you start nesting and don't want to leave a place you have put so much work into even though it may be less than ideal.

The simplest kind of wall to build is one out of deadfall if you are in a wooded area but earth or rocks may have to do in a more arid location. A wall stops or deters both people and animals. It does not even have to be huge. A simple 3-4 foot wall will stop almost all animals while one to deter people will need to be a minimum of 6-8 feet tall. A wall out of deadfall can take advantage of the other trees in your area to use as posts and using 550 Cord you simply tie it together. A wall out of dirt or rock requires much more effort and does not give much more in the way of protection except to gunfire.

WEAPONS

The best weapon in a survival situation is one you already have and are familiar with. Preferably, this should be some sort of firearm. I would have a long gun and at least two identical pistols with some spare parts for both. It could happen that you either don't have a firearm because of local laws or the situation develops so unexpectedly you don't have time to secure your firearms and B.O.B. Bag before you have to get out of Dodge. This section will talk about what to plan and do if you have your weapons with you and also how to make some if you don't. I will also cover how to build weapons that only give once, but give it really well, Booby Traps.

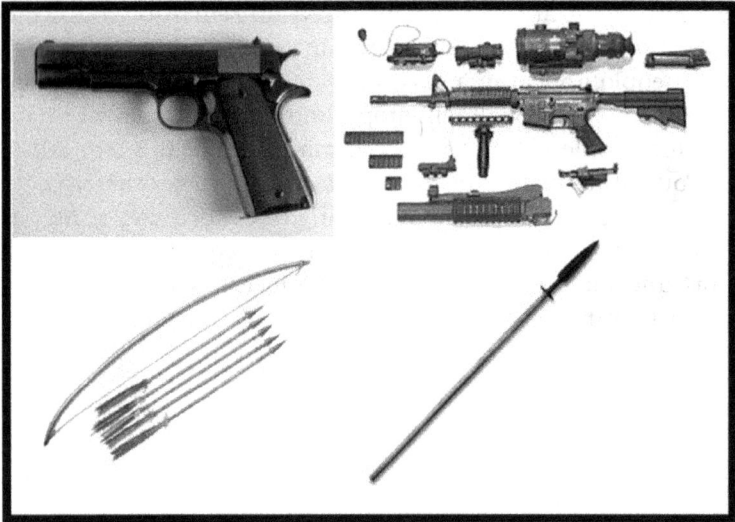

FIREARMS

You will hear as many theories about what the best gun to have is as there are gun enthusiasts in the world. The only advice I will give is that whatever you choose ensure you know how to use it properly and above all how to take care of it. Practice with your weapons as often as you can, daily if possible. If there is a range near your house that lets you conduct CQB firing use it. In any case make sure your weapon's optics and iron sights are both zeroed all the time.

Shooters are generally made not born and just as you can become a good chess player by playing chess, you can become a good shooter by shooting. You will probably not become a competition shooter but that is not the goal, the goal is to become a competent shooter who can hit what he shoots at within likely ranges. Most combat takes place at less than 100 yards and most game is killed ranges not farther than 300 yards so those are the ranges I would practice shooting at. Pistol ranges in combat are even closer, no farther than 50 yards and generally much, much closer even than that.

A gun is a tool just like a wrench or a hammer and if you expect to use it very long you have to take care of it. That means maintenance, maintenance, and more maintenance. You will either get so sick and tired of cleaning your gun you wish for the return of civilization; make weapons maintenance such a part of your day you do it without thinking, or not do it and end up dead. The option of choice is that you make a habit out of it to the point where something feels wrong if you don't do it.

There are actually two different kinds of maintenance you will pull on your weapon; field cleaning, and deliberate cleaning. In field cleaning you strip your weapon down to major assemblies and make sure it is clean enough to fire when you want it to. Deliberate cleaning however, is when you break it down to sub-assemblies and really make it spic and span. Field cleaning is done every day, deliberate cleaning is done at least weekly and after every time you fire it. Cleaning is important not just because gunpowder fouls the weapon but because gunpowder residue is corrosive and will make your weapon rust faster. These cleanings are done regardless of if your weapon of choice is a rifle, a pistol, a slingshot, or a BB gun. The last thing you want to have happen is for your weapon to fail when you need it most. **I cannot emphasize maintenance enough.**

One thing I need to mention is actually killing people. If you watch the news or read too many Dave Grossman books you will get the idea that killing someone is hard. It isn't. What keeps us from being savages is our thin veneer of civilization. That will get wiped away pretty quick if it comes down to a me or them situation. If you are lucky, you will never have to kill anyone. You have to consider that prospect of killing someone and be prepared. Most likely, if you ever do kill anyone it will be with a firearm as well. Sticks, knives, rocks, and bare hands work too though. The advantage with firearms is you don't have to get up in their face to do it, which is safer for you.

LONG GUNS

As guns are tools, there are right ones and wrong ones. The choice is yours to make based on personal considerations. Which weapon you pick depends on many factors including your size and weight, personal dexterity, personal strength, size of the weapon, cost, weight, caliber, ammunition capacity, ammunition abundance, flexibility, modularity, availability of spare parts, and degree of weapons proficiency. That was just a small taste of the items of concern to take into account when selecting a weapon. Personally, I would choose an assault rifle or clone that is good for both close in and medium range work that is not too heavy and is fairly durable.

My personal favorite long gun is the M-4/CAR-15 family mainly because that is the assault rifle I am most familiar with from my military career. It is also probably the most common military-style weapon you will run across in the US after the balloon goes up so that if the weapon does break your likelihood of finding spare parts is much higher. It's advantages are that it is accurate at any realistic range when properly zeroed, has a high capacity magazine, is plentiful on the market, is easy to maintain, and is equally easy to use unless you are a typical ignorant thug in which case you are probably more likely to be attacking a well prepared person than be well prepared yourself.

The next most common military rifle is an AK. I despise AK's. They are cheap, mass-produced, pieces of garbage that are unsuitable for any serious shooting. AK's are heavy, awkward to carry and lack the design features necessary for the addition of any type of optics or accessories that multiply the combat power of the weapon without extensive modification of the weapon itself. They get points for durability and simplicity in general but in my experience an M-4 beats an AK every day of the week and twice on Sundays.

True story, in 2005 because I was a former Drill Sergeant I was selected to spend three months helping to set up the first basic training center for the new Iraqi Army in Tikrit, Iraq. I trained four 3 ½ week long cycles of Iraqi trainees during that time. The human material we got was generally literally *dumb as a bag of hammers*. These guys showed up with just the shirts (read man-dresses) on their back. We had to issue them everything from pen and paper to uniforms and even toothpaste. Only about 20% could read and most had only heard of computers but had never seen one until we inflicted Death by PowerPoint on them in the classroom. We could not get them to understand basic personal hygiene, much less how to use a radio or God forbid, read a map.

Iraqi US Army trainees-June, 2004. The guy with the black hat on the left was one of the Iraqi instructors

We issued the Iraqi trainees brand new, Bulgarian made AK-47's to train with. Now remember, the AK is supposed to be the most rugged weapon in the world, one that a Stone Age savage could pick up and after only 30 minutes of instruction use as proficiently as the spear he was used to carrying. **Wrong**, we actually devoted 1/3 of the course to rifle instruction and range time. None of us expected to be able to train good shooters in that time but we figured, based on our experiences with American trainees that 1 ½ weeks of classroom instruction could keep them from breaking their weapons. **Wrong again**, I saw these guys do things to an AK I would not have thought possible. The most common thing they did was fail to seat the upper receiver cover properly so that when they fired the first round it would pop off and bean them in the eye. The next most common mistake was not seating the magazine properly so they would prepare to fire and the magazine would fall out and hit the ground. I even saw a guy who somehow caused the gas rod guide come loose while he was firing. The AK is anything but idiot-proof. It may also have been just that the material we had was so inferior.

All that aside, you do not have to have an assault rifle. The choice of weapon is entirely up to you and if you are more comfortable with a lever-action Winchester, a Sharps Carbine, or even a hunting rifle that is fine as well. The most important thing is that you be knowledgeable and competent with the weapon you pick. If you are not, someone who is competent with their own is likely to take yours away from you.

I will also discuss weapon accessories. When I mention accessories, I am not speaking of a cool pink pouch with tassels to put your weapon into. I am speaking of additions to your weapon that make it more effective in both self-defense and hunting scenarios. There is no rule that says you cannot kill game with an assault weapon.

SIDEARMS

The next choice you have to make is what do you want for a sidearm, or as I like to call it, the last ditch weapon. You will very rarely use a sidearm but when you do you will really, really need it. It therefore behooves you to pick a sidearm that you can handle and that has enough stopping power that you don't have to shoot an opponent more than twice, and preferably only once.

Any pistol caliber less than .40 is too small and yes that includes the 9mm, which was adopted by the military over the .45 because of its higher capacity magazine. But the military is now moving back to a larger caliber, lower magazine capacity weapon. What difference does it make if you have a 15-round magazine if it takes you six rounds to put a person on the ground? Larger calibers have the decisive advantage that in general one or at most, two rounds is required to put somebody on the ground and out of the fight. An old Vietnam vet I once knew put it this way in regards to the .45. *"You can shoot a man in the pinkie and break his neck because of the force of the round hitting him."*

In general, most men can handle a large-frame pistol such as an M1911 .45, .44 Magnum, or .357 Magnum but these pistols are too large for a woman to get a good grip on so a smaller framed pistol such as a Glock Model 21SF or one of the many small frame SigSauer pistols is in order. Shop around, as with long guns, the choice of weapon is entirely up to you and what suits you the best and what you are most comfortable with.

Some people recommend revolvers with speed-loaders, I don't. The complaint with automatic pistols is that they can jam or misfire more easily. That is true but since you are going to be squared away and pull proper maintenance on your equipment that is not something you have to worry about, is it? Plus, unless you buy an exotic pistol you are talking about weapons with very robust designs. There is a reason the M1911 was the standard issue military sidearm for almost 80 years. The M1911 is built like a brick shithouse and if for some strange reason it does not fire you can beat your opponent to death with it.

FIELD EXPEDIENT WEAPONS

There are four basic weapons that you can fashion just about anywhere in the world where there are trees and rocks. They are the weapons that Neolithic hunters used and they are the ones variations of which were the most common weapons until the introduction of gunpowder in the early 15th Century. The the club, the staff, the spear, and the bow. All are simple to make and can be effective when used with common sense. I will cover each in turn.

THE CLUB

The easiest weapon to get your hands on if you find yourself weaponless is a club. Any handy piece of wood can serve from a short length of timber to a stout stick. Given that most opponents you are likely to face will probably have firearms this is a weapon you want to use from ambush so that you can incapacitate your opponent quickly and then take his gun. You definitely don't want to make this your weapon of choice unless you are fighting zombies and probably not even then. A club can be handy but you want to get your hands on a better weapon as soon as possible as a club is a stopgap weapon at best.

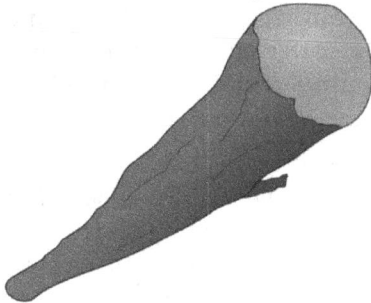

The most suitable club is about arm's length and tapers from the head to the handle. The shape is somewhat important as you want to the head to be heavier than the handle if possible as that will transfer more of the force of your blow to the opponent. Grip is also important. If you have ever hit a baseball without properly choking up on the bat you know the stinging sensation you get in your hands from the bat vibrating, the same thing happens with a club.

In fact, a baseball bat makes a handy club, it aint just for hitting home runs you know.

THE STAFF

A staff, or quarterstaff as they are known amongst people who train with weapons is another of the simple weapons that is easy to come by. Any reasonably straight piece of wood 6-7 feet long and roughly twice as thick as your thumb will do in a pinch. In general a staff should be made of dried hardwood but green wood will work in a pinch, you will just have to make a new one every few weeks as the old one stars to weaken and crack. Try to avoid making a staff out of Pine or Fir as not only are these woods soft, they tend to break spectacularly when put under too much stress. Use Oak, Maple, Hickory, Walnut, or some other deciduous hardwood instead. Hardwood lasts longer and because the wood is denser is better at deflecting edged weapons than other wood. Walnut, and Oak are the best woods unless you run across some Mahogany or Ebony.

It may seem an even worse weapon than the club in some respects but that appreciation would be false. Not only are staffs longer than a club thus extending your reach they can hit harder because they are longer and can be swung faster. Bigger is not always better when it comes to hand melee weapons.

A staff can also be used for things unrelated to fighting. You can use a staff to help steady yourself when walking over rough ground. It can be used to test the ground in areas of uncertain footing and lastly, you can break it up and burn it if you absolutely have to in order to avoid freezing to death.

As a weapon the staff is a step up from a club but it too can be further improved.

THE SPEAR

Take your staff and lash a knife to it and it becomes a spear. Suitable for both hunting and self-defense. Spears are excellent weapons that do not take much beyond courage to wield. The Roman Legionnaire carried everything he owned in a pack attached to his spear (called a Pilum) that was carried resting on his shoulder. A spear was also one of the deadliest weapons available to a dismounted soldier in history. A Roman Pilum was a very specialized weapon and not one you are likely to need unless you encounter hordes of naked Woad-covered Celts running at you through the fens. Not a very likely probability.

To make a spear use the same dimensions of wood as for a staff. A straight branch or piece of wood 6-7 feet long and roughly twice as thick as your thumb. The big difference between a staff and a spear is that a spear has one sharpened end. You can achieve the sharpened end either one of two ways. You can lash a knife or sharp stone to staff or you can whittle down one end of the stick into a sharp point and fire harden it.

If you lash something to one end ensure that you cut a small notch just below the end of the staff to help make the lashing hold more securely. Nothing would be worse than to pigstick one opponent only to find that you unexpectedly have a staff to face the second opponent because your knife was poorly lashed to your spear. A knife is the single most useful survival item you can have because you can use it to make so many other items that you need.

THE BOW

The bow. You would think this one is easy, we all made bows when we were little kids out of a piece of string and a stick we found in the woods. Well, a bow that is to be of any use is anything but easy to make. Don't get me wrong, it can be done, it just takes some discernment in the materials chosen and some serious attention to detail to construct a bow that does anything more than spit an arrow sideways for 30 feet to bounce off a tree.

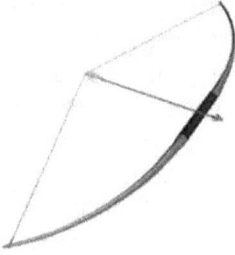

In medieval England Bowyer was a respected trade because it took a lot of skill to build a bow out of a single piece of Yew heartwood that could shoot an arrow 400 yards and was able to penetrate plate armor at 100 yards. There are reports that an English Longbow was powerful enough to drive an arrow far enough through a 6 inch thick oaken door to leave the point of the arrow sticking out on the inside. I challenge anyone to drive even a nail through such a door with one hit from a sledgehammer. Neither you nor I will probably ever be able to build a proper English Longbow. We can though, build a bow powerful enough to take down a deer, rabbit, or man with if we have a little patience and are willing to experiment to find out what works best.

There are actually four components to a bow that we have to concern ourselves with:

1. The bow stave
2. The string
3. The arrow
4. Fletching

Selecting the wood for the bow stave is the most difficult part. You want wood that is strong yet flexible. There is a reason Yew trees are still scarce in England, the heartwood of a Yew was uniquely suited to building longbows. Absent any convenient Yew trees you can use any hardwood. A sapling that is 3-4 inches thick is best because the wood of the growing tree is springier than that of a mature tree.

You will need a piece of wood that is at least as tall as you are to a foot shorter. Try to get one that that has a length of trunk of the required length with no braches growing out of it to avoid knots in the wood. Knots will make your bow brittle and it will probably break with the first shot if not when you are stringing it.

Cut the sapling down and then split it lengthwise so that you have a flat side and a round side, this will be the bow stave. Next strip the bark from the stave and roughly cut it into a bow shape. The ends of the stave should generally be 2/3 as thick as the center. Try to generally follow the grain of the wood as this will help with stability when the bow is finished. Bind both ends of your stave with glue if you have it or cord if you don't. This will keep the ends of the stave from splintering as the wood dries.

Now comes the long part, your stave has to dry. You can make a bow from green wood but it will not last long and the sweat equity you put into it is excessive. Ideally, you should let the wood dry. You do this by tying the middle of the stave, flat side out, to a **straight** object, tree, building frame member, or anything else. This ensures that the stave does not curl incorrectly as it dries. Now wait anywhere from 1-4 weeks depending on the temperature, season, and the time you have available. You can wait as little as 24 hours up to the full month. The longer you wait, the drier the wood and the better the quality of end product you will have.

Once the stave is dry take it down and lay it out. You are now ready to finish the bow stave. Cut two V-shaped notches on the rounded side of the stave about 1½ to 2 inches from the ends for the bowstring and slightly above the center of the stave cut a small notch that will act as an arrow rest. If have suitable material wrap the handle of the bow, it will give you a better grip. You can use leather if you have it but the grip can also be made by wrapping the center with 550 Cord as well.

You are now finally ready to string your bow. Gut and sinew was used in the Middle Ages and you can go this route if you want but a serviceable bowstring can also be made from the inner strands of a piece of 550 Cord. You want your bow string to be 6-8 inches shorter than the overall length of your bow. Now string your bow but don't shoot it yet. Let the strung bow sit overnight to rest the stave. The next day, you can shoot it. Using this method you should get a bow with a range of 100-150 yards that can drop game at 75-125 yards.

Making arrows can be just as difficult as making the bow. You essentially want branches that are about 3 feet long, as thick as your pinkie finger that are as straight as you can get them. The straighter the better as any crookedness will cause them to fly erratically and get you frustrated. The arrows can have fletching or not depending on your skill level and need. Fletching will make them fly straighter when done right and make them fly really strangely when not.

I recommend you start by making un-fletched arrows and try to fletch them when you have the time and opportunity to experiment. Fletching arrows with bird feathers and handmade glue is an art and cannot be adequately explained in this book.

A last tip on arrows is that if you do not have arrowheads, don't try to make them like the Indians did, that is very time consuming. A simple method of putting a head on your arrow is to whittle the wood down to a point and fire harden it. That should be more than sufficient for survival needs until you can acquire a more modern weapon. In a long-term survival situation and when ammo is precious a bow can be a useful adjunct for hunting that lets you conserve firearm ammunition for when you really need it.

BOOBY TRAPS

Booby traps, or mechanical ambushes, as the military calls them are like little guards that never sleep on duty and do their job right every time given a minimum of love and attention. In fact, you could say they do them too well since they are likely to catch you if you are careless around them. I will not cover explosive booby traps in this book since Demolitions (demo) is a field all its own and somebody messing with demo who does not know what they are doing, or even worse, has a little knowledge will probably only succeed in getting themselves killed. I will however, say one thing about demo, **unless you are properly trained, don't touch it**; I don't care how easy the movies make it look, it ain't.

Remember that Booby Traps are not generally designed to kill people, they are supposed to wound or maim them. This sounds harsh at first but it makes perfect sense according the calculus of combat. If you kill somebody the body can be safely ignored until the battle is over. If you wound somebody not only do you take that person out of the equation, depending on the severity of the wound you also take 1-4 other people out of the fight to care for that one wounded individual. Therefore the goal of most booby traps is to wound your opponent although killing them is generally good too. That being said, there are several traps you can make or improvise that do not require things that go boom. They are all simple and if emplaced properly can add to your security. Most booby traps, explosive or not, only require minimal maintenance but they all require some maintenance if they are to be in place for any length of time.

Traps have two purposes one material and the other psychological. The material is obvious, to kill or incapacitate an attacker or disable their vehicles. The psychological is not so obvious. Traps have an insidious effect on people because they are unexpected. If an opponent is in an area where there are traps they must be on heightened alert. Maintaining alertness is very draining and quickly takes a toll on the mind and body. Traps also produce a constant state of fear because it is unknown where they are and when or if the traps will go off wounding or killing someone. For the purposes of deterrence, a trap that causes a non-fatal maiming wound is better than one that kills a person outright, unless you are willing to let the body stay there as a warning to others that you are not to be messed with.

The simplest form of trap is the Pungi/Tiger Pit, the most difficult traps involve significant manpower but can do quite a bit of damage. All traps involve some amount of effort that is not directly related to survival, unless you are building a trap for hunting, which is covered in Chapter 3. However, if you find yourself having to laager or stay in one area for any length of time due to illness or injury to a member of your party and there are potentially hostile groups in the area then traps are something worth considering.

The placement of traps, must be planned, you don't just go out and find a good spot and put traps in at random. The US Army uses a minefield Record Card (DA Form 1355 in Appendix B) to record minefields but it or something similar can just as easily be used to plan and record the locations of the traps you emplace. Planning and recording your trap scheme does two things, it ensures your scheme is rational and it helps to keep you or someone in your party from falling into your own traps.

You will be amazed at what you can build with a shovel, an axe, some rope, a nail or two, and imagination. You can do anything from immobilize an opponent to kill and injure them depending on the trap you decide to build.

PUNGI PIT

The Pungi Pit originally got its name during World War II when they were used by the Japanese during the island fighting campaigns in the Pacific. They were used again by the Viet Cong in the 1960's during the Vietnam War. When constructed properly the Pungi Pit is not only an effective trap it also plays a psychological role as people who fall into it die in a pretty horrific manner. US Army jungle boots are constructed with a thin steel plate all along the bottom of the sole because of these traps.

This is a deceptively simple trap to construct. It is essentially a circular or rectangular pit dug between 2 and 3 feet deep perpendicularly across a trail or other path. Inside the pit sharpened stakes (Pungi stakes) are set into the ground with the points up. The stakes are placed close enough together that anyone stepping into the pit will step on at least one of the stakes. Bamboo works best for the stakes if it is available because bamboo resists softening when it gets wet. Amazingly, bamboo is more common than you think in North America because it has become popular as an ornamental plant. But if no bamboo is available the stakes can be fashioned from other wood or even metal, regular commercial rebar works best for metal stakes since all you have to do is sharpen one end.

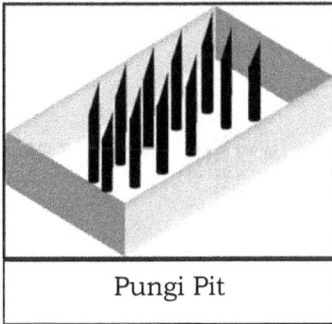

Pungi Pit

Once the pit is dug and the stakes are positioned a lightweight framework is built that is placed over the top of the trap and then camouflaged to fit the surrounding ground. A well-constructed Pungi Pit is indistinguishable from the ground to either side until you step on it.

Traditionally the Pungi stakes are also smeared with human or animal excrement to facilitate infection of the wounds caused. Human excrement is preferred because it carries more pathogens that will make people sick.

Generally it is not the stake through the foot that kills someone who steps in a Pungi Pit, it is the raging infection that takes hold from the feces being forced into the wound. This leads to a lingering and painful death. It is the nature of the wounds and the death that follows that gives Pungi Pits their psychological edge.

Pungi Pit

Image ©Paul Marquis and used with permission
http://www.echo23marines6569.org/files/punji.jpg

SHOTGUN SHELL TOE POPPER

The Toe Popper is so named because that is exactly what it is designed to do, pop people's toes off. It is not designed to kill, it is rather designed to maim and remove people out of the fight. It is deceptively easy to build and if a few simple precautions are taken it can last for months without being checked.

Even if you don't have a shotgun in your B.O.B. Bag, it might be a good idea to have at least one 25 round box of 12 Gauge or .410 Gauge #4 Shot shotgun shells with you. They can come in handy for several things and this trap is one of the most useful. Ensure that if you do use shotgun shells they are the newer plastic-hulled shells instead of paper-hulled so that the cartridge and powder does not become damp and fail to fire.

First, I prefer #4 Birdshot instead of Buckshot for this trap because they tend to do the most debilitating damage without immediately killing the target. But believe me, you ain't thinking about shooting anybody after your foot has been shredding by a couple dozen shotgun pellets. This trap can also be made with rifle or pistol cartridges. It requires a little more in the way of equipment than a Pungi pit but is much smaller and much easier to conceal as well. The equipment needed to construct this trap is:

- Shotgun shell or other cartridge
- Small piece of appropriate diameter pipe or tubing
- Two small boards
- Small roofing nail or finishing brad
- 550 cord

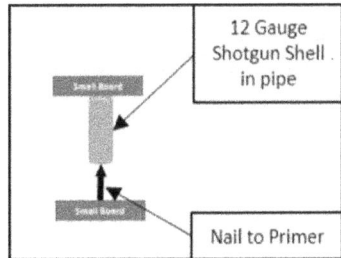

To construct this trap you take the small board and drive the nail through the board so that the tip of the nail is showing through on the other side. Then you must affix the pipe to the board such that the protruding nail is in the center of the pipe. Place the shot shell or cartridge in the pipe primer side down so that at least ¼ inch of the cartridge is sticking above the pipe. The take the second board and place it flat across the top of the cartridge.

This contraption is then placed into a small hole in your location of choice. Fill in the hole and camouflage it so that it is indistinguishable from the surrounding terrain.

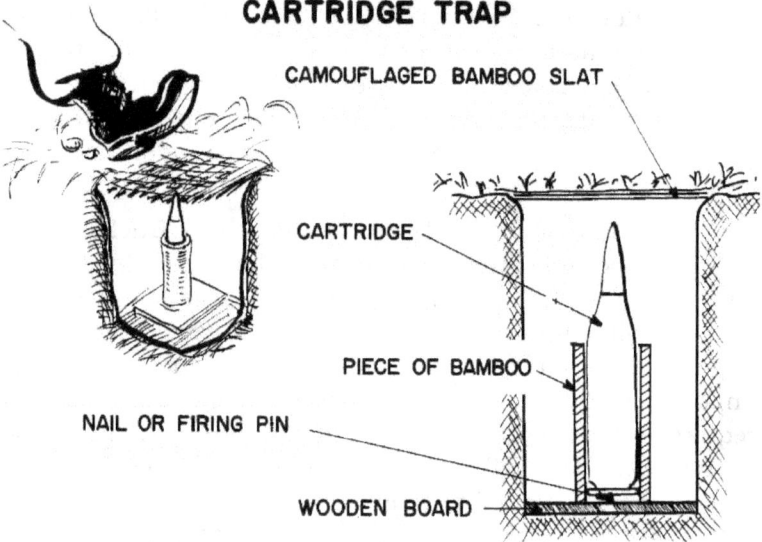

CARTRIDGE TRAP

CAMOUFLAGED BAMBOO SLAT

CARTRIDGE

PIECE OF BAMBOO

NAIL OR FIRING PIN

WOODEN BOARD

Gun Cartridge Toe Popper

Image ©Paul Marquis and used with permission http://www.echo23marines6569.org/files/cartridge_trap .jpg

DEADFALL

The deadfall can come in many forms, some you have probably seen and others you have not. In its essence, a deadfall trap is one in which a heavy object is suspended or put under tension such that when the trap is sprung it swings into the area of the trigger and does damage to whoever or whatever is there. Remember the scene in *The Empire Strikes Back* where the Stormtrooper gets crushed between two logs? That is the kind of trap I am talking about here just generally not as elaborate as what the Ewoks make. As with all trap types, only your imagination and abilities limit what you can with this kind of trap.

To make a trap of this sort with a heavy log is both time and manpower intensive and additionally such a trap is difficult to camouflage as the log must have a free swing route unless it is so huge that it becomes impractical for 1-4 people to construct. There are other more profitable traps of this type to build than to try and recreate *Star Wars*.

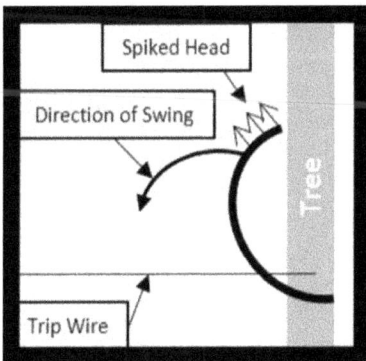

A common trap of this type in Vietnam was using a green sapling and tying one end off to a tree while bending the other back to put tension on it with a wire release. The moving end would often have a bamboo frame with spikes on it that would embed themselves in whoever tripped the trap. As with Pungi pits, human feces is a good addition to this kind of trap because it will make any wounds that are not immediately fatal fester and get infected.

You can make a variation of this trap that swings downward using its own weight if you cannot find suitable saplings. The advantage of putting such a trap up in the tree instead of on the ground are that it is easier to camouflage such a trap and more importantly, most people are looking at ground level instead of over their heads if they are in a hostile environment. All traps of this type can also be rigged for command execution. That is, instead of having a wire of string crossing a trail they can be set up so that a defender sets them off at a time of their choosing. This is a good thing because you can let one or two opponents past the trap and then set it off and maybe catch their leader in the trap. At a minimum, such a tactic will sow confusion and instill fear among your opponents and make them easier to defeat or drive off.

CHAPTER 7 – BASIC FIELD FIRST AID

"It is a kingly act to assist the fallen."
Ovid (1st Century Roman Poet)

A skill that will undoubtedly be necessary in any survival situation from the end of the world to an accident on a weekend camping trip is First Aid. In a survival situation there are two very good reasons to be knowledgeable in First Aid. One, it could very well be the difference between life and death; second, in the absence of modern medicine minor wounds can very easily be debilitating or even deadly. A little tidbit to think on is that until the advent of modern medicine broken limbs were very often fatal. Think on that for a minute. In today's world a broken leg or arm is not considered serious by most people and if they think on it at all they think of a trip to the doctor, an x-ray, and a cast. Yet 125 years ago a broken limb was life threatening.

One section I do not go into great depth in in the book is First Aid. I am not a qualified EMT and do not want to make the mistake of putting some advice in here that is wrong and can make an injured person worse than if you do nothing. I have put in the most basic stuff that I have used and know works but recommend that for first aid you do two things.

1. Seek out and get training on first aid from a competent source. I highly recommend getting first aid certified by the Red Cross at a minimum.

2. Get a reference book written by subject matter experts that are infinitely more knowledgeable than I am on the things to do and avoid if someone in your party gets injured. I recommend _The Survival Medicine Handbook: A Guide for When Help is Not on the Way_ by Joseph and Amy Alton, which is available for purchase on Amazon and at many other book outlets.

FIELD EXPEDIENT MEDICINES

There are several common plants that are useful as medicines. The section below is taken directly from US Army FM 21-76 Survival. These are the most useful herbal remedies readily available in a survival situation. There are plenty more if you take the time to research them before the end of the world.

- **Tannin.**
    - ○ *Medical uses.*
        - ▪ Burns, diarrhea, dysentery, skin problems, and parasites. A Tannin solution helps prevent infection and aids in healing.
    - ○ *Sources.*
        - ▪ Found in the outer bark of all trees, acorns, Banana plants, common Plantain, Strawberry leaves, and Blackberry stems.
    - ○ *Preparation.*
        - ▪ Place crushed outer bark, acorns, or leaves in water.
        - ▪ Leach out the tannin by soaking or boiling.
            - • Increase tannin content by longer soaking time.
            - • Replace depleted material with fresh bark/plants to increase the amount of Tannin in the solution.
    - ○ *Treatments.*
        - ▪ Burns.
            - • Moisten a bandage with cooled tannin tea.
            - • Apply as a compress to burned area.
            - • Pour the cooled tea on burned areas to ease pain.
        - ▪ Diarrhea, dysentery, and worms.

- Drink strong tea solution (may promote voiding of worms).
  - Skin problems (dry rashes and fungal infections).
    - Apply cool compresses or soak the affected part to relieve itching and promote healing.
  - Lice and insect bites.
    - Wash affected areas with tea to ease itching.
- **Salicin/Salicylic Acid.**
  - *Medical uses.*
    - Aches, colds, fever, inflammation, pain, sprains, and sore throat (active ingredient of aspirin).
  - *Sources.*
    - Willow and Aspen tree
  - *Preparation.*
    - Gather twigs, buds, or cambium layer (soft, moist layer between the outer bark and the wood) of Willow or Aspen.
    - Prepare a tea
    - Make a poultice.
      - Crush the plant or stems.
      - Make a pulpy mass.
  - *Treatments.*
    - Chew on twigs, buds, or cambium for symptom relief.
    - Drink as a tea for colds and sore throat.
    - Use a warm, moist poultice for aches and sprains.
      - Apply pulpy mass over injury.
      - Hold in place with a dressing.
- **Common Cattail.**
  - *Medical uses.*
    - Wounds, sores, boils, inflammations, burns, and an excellent food source.
  - *Source.*
    - Cattail plant found in marshes
  - *Preparation.*

- Pound roots into a pulpy mass for a poultice.
- Cook and eat green bloom spikes.
- Collect yellow pollen for flour substitute.
- Peel and eat tender shoots (raw or cooked).
- *Treatments.*
  - Apply as a poultice to affected area.
  - Use plant for food, vitamins, and minerals.

EVALUATE A CASUALTY

A key thing pounded into you by the army in regards to First Aid is made up of the steps to evaluate a casualty. The great part about learning First Aid this way is the steps move in order from most important to least important. As in, if you don't do the things on the list first it does not matter if you do the later things because your casualty will be dead anyway.

As you go through the eight steps they are a series of what are essentially **Yes/No** questions. If the answer to the question is no move on to the next step. If the answer however is yes, then it references what you should do as First Aid before moving on to the next step. For example, step four is to check for shock and it lists the symptoms of shock. If your casualty has no symptoms great, move on. If they do then treat the casualty for shock before moving on to the next step.

The Eight Steps to
Evaluate a Casualty are The mnemonic
device to remember these steps is:
Rub Both Balls Softly For Better Head

1. *Responsiveness*   **– RUB**
2. *Breathing*   **– BOTH**
3. *Bleeding*   **– BALLS**
4. *Shock*   **– SOFTLY**
5. *Fractures*   **– FOR**
6. *Burns*   **– BETTER**
7. *Head Injury*   **– HEAD**
8. *Heat Injury/Cold Injury*

0. CHECK FOR HAZARDS

Quickly evaluate your immediate surroundings and the casualty for obvious, immediate, life-threatening hazards. Examples of such hazards include burning vehicles, explosion, gunfire, fire, and electrical wires touching or very near the casualty. If you and the casualty are in a relatively safe location and the casualty is not being burned, continue your evaluation. If the casualty is being burned, eliminate the source of the burn taking care to prevent being injured yourself, especially if you must remove an electrical wire.

If an immediate, life-threatening hazard (such as a burning building) is present, remove the casualty to a place of safety then continue your evaluation.

1. CHECK FOR RESPONSIVENESS

Calmly ask in a loud voice, "Are you okay?" or some similar question that demands a response from the casualty. If he does not answer, gently shake or tap them on the shoulder and repeat the question. If the casualty responds, ask the casualty for information, (Where do you hurt? Are you hit? etc.) Their information will be useful, but continue to evaluate the casualty in a systematic method since the injury that hurts the most may not be the injury that needs to be treated first.

If the casualty is not responsive continue your evaluation.

2. CHECK FOR DIFFICULTY BREATHING

If the casualty is responsive, evaluate them for airway obstruction (universal choking sign, difficulty in breathing). If the casualty has good air exchange, continue your evaluation. If the casualty has poor or no air exchange, expel the obstruction and continue your evaluation. If the casualty is not responsive (unconscious), evaluate their respirations by:

(1) Looking for rise and fall of the casualty's chest.

(2) Listening for breathing by placing your ear about one inch above the casualty's mouth and nose.

(3) Feeling for breathing by placing your hand or cheek about one inch above the casualty's mouth and nose.

If the casualty has good air exchange, continue your evaluation. If the casualty is not breathing, open their airway and perform Rescue Breathing. If the casualty resumes breathing, continue your evaluation.

CAUTION
Do not turn the casualty onto their back or move the head and trunk until you have checked for a back and/or neck injury.

3. CHECK FOR BLEEDING

Check the casualty for bloody clothing, pools of blood, spurts of blood, entry and exit wounds, etc.

If there is no serious bleeding, continue the evaluation. If bleeding is present, stop the evaluation and begin treatment as appropriate (see Page 174).

4. CHECK FOR SHOCK

Shock can be just as life threatening as bleeding out. You can treat all the casualties other wounds/conditions and think they are doing fine and if they go into shock they can die anyway. Always treat a fresh casualty for shock regardless of if they display symptoms

- Shock can be caused by injury or wounds or bleeding.
- Shock can interfere with the normal flow of blood through the body.
- Shock **can** cause death.

The following are the signs and symptoms of shock:

Check the casualty for clammy skin, pale or blotchy skin, bluish skin (especially around the mouth), nausea and/or vomiting, severe loss of blood, increased breathing

WARNING
UNLESS THERE IS IMMEDIATE LIFE-THREATENING DANGER, DO NOT MOVE A CASUALTY WHO HAS A SUSPECTED BACK OR NECK INJURY.

rate, unusual thirst, restlessness, and mental confusion. If shock is not present, continue your evaluation. If shock is present, stop the evaluation and treat for shock (see Page 184). Splint leg fractures **before** elevating the legs as a treatment for shock.

5. CHECK FOR FRACTURES

Check for cuts and bruises in and around the neck and back area, paralysis, numbness in extremities, pain or tenderness around the spinal column, severe head injury (deformed skull or visible brain tissue or skull fragments), and unusual positioning of the head, neck, and/or back. If no spinal injury is suspected, continue your evaluation. If a neck or back injury is suspected, immobilize the casualty by doing the following:

(1) Tell the casualty not to move.

(2) For a back injury, place padding under the natural arch of the casualty's back. Roll or fold the padding to conform to the shape of the arch.

(3) For a neck injury, place a roll of cloth under the casualty's neck and immobilize the neck by putting boots (filled with dirt, sand, etc.) on both sides of the head. Rocks can be used, if necessary, on the sides of the casualty's head provided they are padded.

After immobilizing the casualty, check their arms and legs for open or closed fractures.

An open fracture is a broken bone that breaks (pierces) the overlying skin.

(1) Look for bleeding.

(2) Look for bone sticking through the skin.

(3) Ask a conscious casualty to tell you where there is pain or tenderness or which areas cannot be moved.

A closed fracture is a broken bone that does not break the overlying skin. Look for:

(a) Swelling.

(b) Discoloration.

(c) Deformity.

(d) Unusual body position.

(e) Presence, quality, and rate of distal pulses beyond the suspected fracture site.

If no fracture or massive wound is found, continue your evaluation. If a fracture is found, treat the fracture (see Page 188) before continuing.

6. CHECK FOR BURNS

Burns often cause extreme pain, scarring, or even death. Proper treatment will minimize further injury.

The source of the burn (electricity, etc.) must be eliminated before any evaluation or treatment of the casualty can occur. Checking for burns involves checking for singed clothing, and for reddened, blistered, or charred skin. If no burns are found, continue your evaluation. If burns are found, stop the evaluation and begin treatment

7. CHECK FOR HEAD INJURY

Usually, serious skull fractures and brain injuries occur together; however, it is possible to receive a serious brain injury without a skull fracture. The brain is a very delicate organ. When it is injured, the casualty may exhibit a number of signs and/or symptoms.

Check the casualty for unequal pupils, fluid leaking from the ears or nose, mental confusion (cannot tell you the date when asked, etc.), slurred speech, recent unconsciousness, loss of memory, dizziness or difficulty in walking, nausea, sleepiness, and twitching or convulsions. If no head injury is found, continue your evaluation. If the casualty has a suspected concussion, position the casualty in a sitting position, on their side, or on their stomach with their head turned to one side to avoid aspiration in the case of vomiting. If the casualty is having convulsions, support the head and neck and maintain an open airway. Continue to watch for signs that would require: performance of Rescue Breathing, treatment for shock, or control of bleeding. If the casualty has an open head wound, treat the head wound before continuing.

8. CHECK FOR COLD/HEAT INJURY

If the casualty has been working in a hot environment or has been working hard, check for signs and symptoms of heat cramps (painful contractions of the limbs or abdomen and heavy perspiration), heat exhaustion (heavy perspiration, pale and clammy skin, weakness or faintness, and dizziness), and heatstroke (little or no perspiration, hot and flushed skin, nausea, mental confusion, convulsions, and possible unconsciousness).

If no heat injury is present, continue your evaluation.

If the casualty has a heat injury begin First Aid for the injury(see Page 200).

If the casualty has been exposed to freezing weather, check for blanched skin, yellowish or waxy-looking skin, numb areas, and frozen (solid feeling) tissue.

If no cold injury is present, continue your evaluation.

If a cold injury is found begin First Aid for a cold injury(see Page 204).

RENDERING IMMEDIATE FIRST AID

The procedures below are for immediate first aid to assist an injured person and get them out of danger of immediate death. In a survival situation you will not be able to evacuate someone to a hospital for further treatment. If you are lucky one of your party members will be a doctor. If you are unlucky you will have to give such treatment yourself. For details on that treatment get trained beforehand and have a suitable reference available such as *The Survival Medicine Handbook: A Guide for When Help is Not on the Way* by Joseph and Amy Alton.

FIRST AID FOR BLEEDING OF AN EXTREMITY.

INTRODUCTION

A casualty who is losing blood rapidly (hemorrhaging) may die unless the bleeding is stopped. Bleeding from an extremity (arm or leg) can usually be controlled by applying a dressing and bandage, applying manual pressure, elevating the injured limb, and (if necessary) applying a pressure dressing. If these methods do not control the bleeding, a tourniquet may be required. (NOTE: The procedures in this lesson are used to control bleeding from an upper arm, forearm, thigh, or lower leg.)

A dressing is the material that is placed directly over the wound. The dressing absorbs some of the blood and helps to cause a clot to form. The clot helps to "plug" the wound and stop the bleeding. The dressing also helps to prevent further contamination of the wound and provides protection to the injured area.

A bandage is the material used to hold (secure) the dressing in place so the dressing will not slip off the wound. The ends of the bandage are called the "tails."

You should have at least two Israeli Field Dressings in your B.O.B. Bag. The Israeli Field Dressing combines a

173

traditional field dressing with a pressure dressing and tourniquet hen needed in one sterile package.

EXPOSE THE WOUND

Expose the wound by tearing, cutting, and/or lifting the casualty's clothing and other material away from the wound. The entire wound area is exposed so that you can see the full extent of the injury. If clothing is stuck to the wound area, do not try to remove that part of the clothing from the wound. Do not try to remove objects from the wound.

Avoid causing additional damage to the wound. If the wound was caused by a bullet, shrapnel, or other projectile, look for both an entry wound and an exit wound.

APPLY AND SECURE FIELD DRESSING

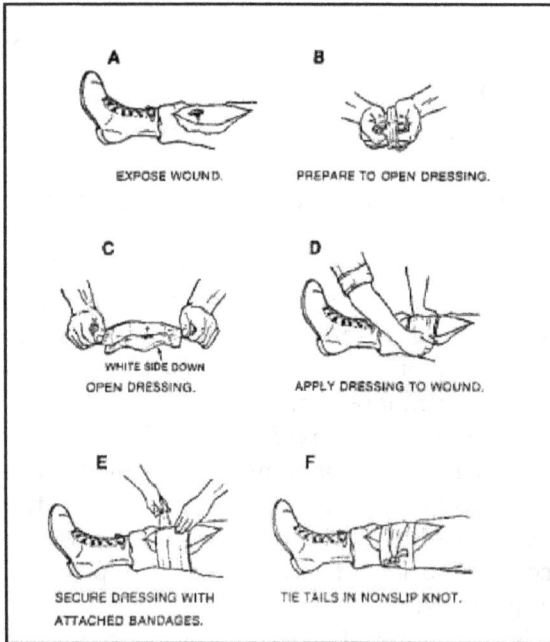

A — EXPOSE WOUND.

B — PREPARE TO OPEN DRESSING.

C — WHITE SIDE DOWN. OPEN DRESSING.

D — APPLY DRESSING TO WOUND.

E — SECURE DRESSING WITH ATTACHED BANDAGES.

F — TIE TAILS IN NONSLIP KNOT.

APPLYING AND SECURING A FIELD DRESSING

After you have exposed the wound, remove a field dressing

Tear the plastic envelope and remove its contents. Twist the paper wrapper until it breaks or tear it open.

Grasp the folded bandages/tails with both hands.

Hold the field dressing

above the exposed wound with the white side of the dressing material toward the wound.

Pull on the tails so that the dressing opens and flattens.

CAUTION
Do not touch the white, sterile side of the field dressing

Place the dressing over the wound. Remember, the white side of the dressing goes next to the wound.

Use one hand to hold the dressing in place. If the casualty is conscious, you can have them hold the dressing in place while you secure it.

Wrap one of the bandages around the injured limb with your free hand. As you wrap, cover one of the exposed sides of the dressing with the bandage. (The bandage can usually be wrapped around the limb more than once.) Bring the tail back over the dressing.

Wrap the other bandage around the injured limb in the opposite direction. As you wrap, cover the remaining exposed side of the dressing with the bandage. Bring the tail back to the dressing.

Tie the tails into a nonslip knot over the outer edge of the dressing, not over the wound itself. (Tying the knot over the wound could cause additional injury to the wound site.) The tails should be tight enough so that the dressing will not slip, but not tight enough to interfere with blood circulation.

Check the circulation below (distal to) the bandage. If the skin below the bandage becomes cool to the touch, bluish, or numb, the bandage may be too tight and interfering with circulation. Loosen and retie the tails, then check the circulation again.

CAUTION
Do not remove the dressing from the wound. Removing the dressing would interfere with any clot that had begun to form.

APPLY MANUAL PRESSURE

Apply direct pressure over the dressing with your hand. This pressure will help to compress the damaged blood vessels and control the bleeding. Maintain this pressure for five to ten minutes. If the casualty is conscious and can follow instructions, you can have them apply the manual pressure themself.

WARNING
Examine the injured extremity for fractures (visible broken bone, deformity of the limb, etc.). If a fracture is suspected, do not elevate the wound until the limb has been splinted

ELEVATE THE WOUND

Elevate the injured limb above the level of the casualty's heart. Elevating the limb will help to decrease the bleeding. For example, an injured leg can be raised by placing the foot on a pack, log, rock, or other object. An injured forearm can be elevated by placing the forearm on the casualty's chest if he is lying on their back or by having the casualty place their arm on top of their head if he is sitting up. Elevating the injured limb and applying manual pressure should be done at the same time when no fracture is involved.

APPLY A PRESSURE DRESSING

WARNING
A pressure dressing is applied only to a wound on an extremity.

CAUTION
The field dressing is not removed; the bandages are not loosened and retied. Moving the dressing would interfere with any clot which had begun to form

If blood continues to seep from the dressing even after you secure the dressing, apply manual pressure, and elevate the wound (if applicable), then a pressure dressing is needed to help stop the bleeding. The objective of applying a pressure dressing is to stop bleeding, not to stop all blood circulation below the wound. (Stopping all blood circulation would endanger the body tissue located below the bandage since these tissues would not receive the oxygen and nutrients carried by the blood.)

Use the included pressure device or place a wad of material on top of the dressing and directly over the wound. The wad can be made by folding a rag, material torn from clothing, or any other bulky material.

Place a bandage over the wad and wrap the bandage tightly around the wound. The bandage can be a triangular bandage folded into a cravat, handkerchief, sock, strip of cloth torn from a shirt, or other similar material. Narrow materials like shoestrings should not be used since they are likely to damage blood vessels and nerve tissue.

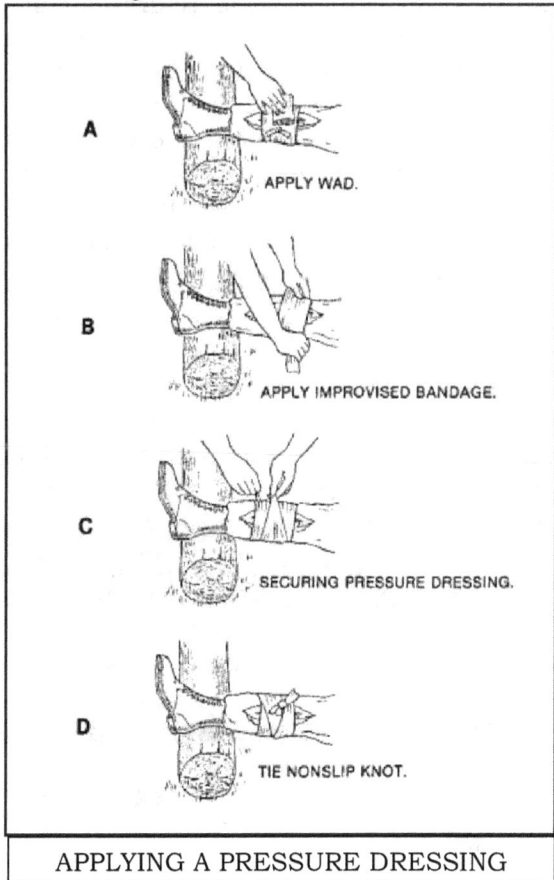

A. APPLY WAD.

B. APPLY IMPROVISED BANDAGE.

C. SECURING PRESSURE DRESSING.

D. TIE NONSLIP KNOT.

APPLYING A PRESSURE DRESSING

Tie the ends of the bandage to secure the padding. A nonslip knot should be **tied directly over the wound**. The

177

bandage should be tight enough so that only the tip of one finger can be inserted under the bandage. Do not tie the bandage so tight that it cuts off all blood circulation.

Tie the ends of the bandage to secure the padding. A nonslip knot should be **tied directly over the wound**. The bandage should be tight enough so that only the tip of one finger can be inserted under the bandage. Do not tie the bandage so tight that it cuts off all blood circulation.

Check the circulation below the pressure dressing. If the skin below the bandage becomes cool to the touch, bluish, or numb, the pressure dressing may be too tight. If so, loosen and retie the tails. (The pressure dressing can be loosened and retied without disturbing the blood clot forming under the field dressing.)

Apply manual pressure over the pressure dressing.

If use of a pressure dressing controls the bleeding, proceed to check the casualty for other injuries. If the wound continues to bleed profusely, apply a tourniquet.

APPLY A TOURNIQUET

A tourniquet is placed around an arm (upper arm or forearm) or leg (thigh or lower leg) in order to stop the flow of the blood below the tourniquet. It is used only when the amount of blood being lost endangers the casualty's life and the bleeding cannot be stopped by the application of a field dressing, manual pressure, elevation, and pressure

WARNING
A tourniquet is applied only to an upper arm, forearm, thigh, or lower leg. It is not used for wounds to the head, neck, or trunk or for a wound on the hand or foot.

dressing.

GATHER MATERIALS FOR MAKING A TOURNIQUET

If you are using an Israeli field dressing the integral pressure device can simply be twisted and secured with the tail of the bandage to make a tourniquet. A one hand tourniquet can be used by placing it above the injury but not on a joint and pulling the cord tight until blood flow stops. If you do not have an Israeli field dressing or one hand tourniquet use the methods outlined below to fashion a tourniquet.

Tourniquet Band

You will need a band of strong, pliable material which is at least two inches wide when folded. A folded muslin bandage (usually called a cravat), a folded handkerchief, or a folded strip of clothing will do. <u>Do not</u> use wire or shoestrings for a tourniquet band. A two-inch wide tourniquet will protect the tissue beneath the tourniquet when it is tightened. If a very narrow tourniquet is used, the nerves and blood vessels beneath the tourniquet may be seriously damaged.

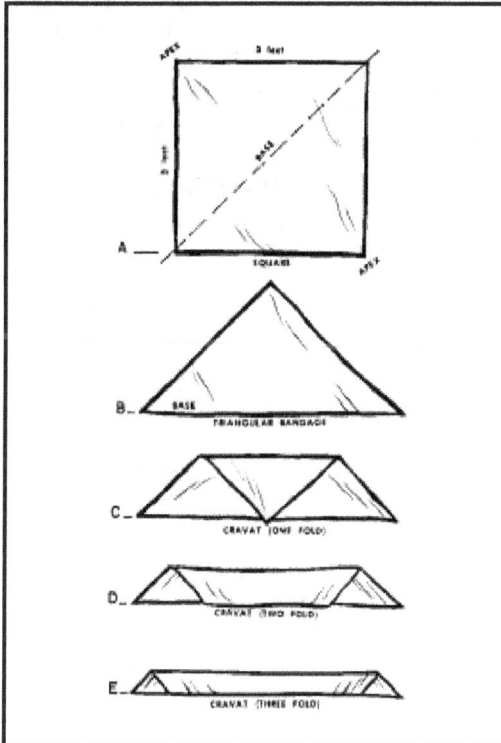

FOLDING A MUSLIN BANDAGE OR A SQUARE OF MATERIAL INTO A TOURNIQUET BAND

Rigid Object

A rigid object, usually a stick, is needed to tighten the tourniquet.

Securing Materials

Material is needed to secure the rigid object once the tourniquet has been tightened. A piece of cloth such as is used for the tourniquet will do. If the tourniquet band is long enough, the tails can be used to secure the rigid object.

Padding

Padding is placed between the limb and the tourniquet band to protect the skin from being pinched and twisted when the band is tightened. Soft, smooth material should be used for padding. The casualty's shirt sleeve or trouser leg can be used as padding.

APPLY A TOURNIQUET TO A WOUND

WARNING

A tourniquet is used only when the amount of blood being lost endangers the casualty's life and all other methods of controlling the bleeding have failed. Since the tourniquet will stop blood circulation, the body tissues below (distal to) the tourniquet will not receive oxygen and nutrients. The limb part located below the tourniquet may later need to be amputated.

The tourniquet should be placed two to four inches above the edge of the wound (between the wound and the heart). If the wound is just below the elbow or knee, the tourniquet should be placed above the joint and as close to the joint as possible. **Do not** place the tourniquet over the elbow or knee.

Place padding around the limb where the tourniquet will be applied. If the casualty's shirt sleeve or pants leg is covering the tourniquet site, smooth the shirt or pants material and apply the tourniquet over the clothing.

Place the tourniquet band material around the tourniquet site.

Tie the band with a half knot. (A

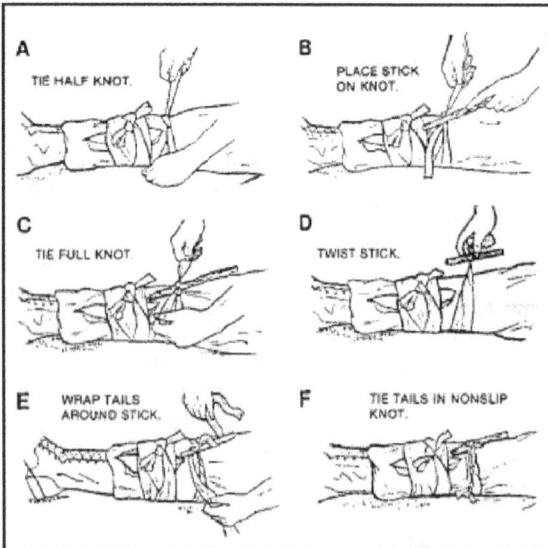

A TIE HALF KNOT.
B PLACE STICK ON KNOT.
C TIE FULL KNOT.
D TWIST STICK.
E WRAP TAILS AROUND STICK.
F TIE TAILS IN NONSLIP KNOT.

APPLYING A TOURNIQUET

half knot is the same as the first part of tying a shoe.)

Place the rigid object on top of the half knot.

Tie a full knot over the rigid object.

Twist the rigid object either clockwise or counterclockwise until the tourniquet is tight and the bright red bleeding has stopped. (Bright red blood is from a severed artery. Darker blood is from a vein. Dark blood may continue to ooze even after the tourniquet has been properly applied.)

Wrap the tails of the tourniquet band around the end of the rigid object so the rigid object will not untwist.

Wrap the tails around the limb (arm or leg) and tie the tails so that the rigid object stays secure.

If the rigid object cannot be secured with the tails of the tourniquet band, wrap a piece of material around the limb **below** the tourniquet, wrap the material around one end of the rigid object so that the tourniquet will not unwind, and tie the tails of the material in a nonslip knot. (**NOTE**: The rigid object is secured below the tourniquet so the securing material will not interfere with blood circulation above the tourniquet.)

WARNING
Do not loosen the tourniquet once it is in place and has stopped the blood flow. If it is loosened, the wound will start to bleed again. The additional blood loss may cause the casualty to go into shock, which could be fatal. A tourniquet should only be loosened by medical personnel.

WARNING
Bleeding from the amputation of part of a hand or part of a foot can be controlled through pressure dressing, manual pressure, and elevation and does not require the application of a tourniquet..

APPLY A TOURNIQUET TO AN AMPUTATION

An upper arm, forearm, thigh, or lower leg that has been completely severed (amputated) requires a tourniquet. A tourniquet is to be applied to an arm or leg that has been amputated even if the stump is not bleeding. The absence of blood is due to the body's normal defenses (constriction of blood vessels), but the stump will begin to bleed profusely when the blood vessels relax.

The tourniquet should be applied two to four inches above the edge of the amputation. If the limb has been amputated just below the knee or elbow, apply the tourniquet just above the joint. **Do not** attempt to control the bleeding by applying field and pressure dressings prior to applying the tourniquet.

If possible, place padding around the tourniquet site.

Place the tourniquet band around the tourniquet site. Use the rigid object to tighten the band and stop the blood flow. Then secure the rigid object to prevent the tourniquet from loosening. The procedures are the same as given in the previous paragraphs.

After the tourniquet has been applied, place a dressing made of soft, absorbent material over the end of the stump and secure the dressing with bandages. The dressing will help prevent additional contamination of the wound and will help to protect the wound from additional injury.

MARK THE CASUALTY

Write a "T" on the casualty's forehead using a pen, the casualty's blood, mud, or other substance. The "T" alerts other people that a tourniquet has been applied. Also include the time and date the tourniquet was applied, if possible. This information is important to anybody else who treats the casualty.

FIRST AID TO PREVENT OR CONTROL SHOCK

1. INTRODUCTION

Shock occurs when the tissues or organs of the body do not receive enough oxygen and nutrients from the blood circulatory system. There are several causes of shock. On the battlefield, low blood volume (hypovolemic) shock will be the primary type of shock treated by buddy-aid. Hypovolemic shock is usually caused by severe bleeding, but it can also be caused by a severe loss of body fluids from other causes (vomiting, diarrhea, excessive sweating, severe burns, etc.). Other types of shock can be caused by infections; by allergic reactions to drugs, food, or insect bites; and by heart failure. Shock, if not properly treated, can result in death.

When treating a casualty, assume that shock is present or will occur shortly. By waiting until actual signs/symptoms of shock are noticeable, the rescuer may jeopardize the casualty's life.

2. IDENTIFY THE SIGNS AND SYMPTOMS OF SHOCK

Signs and symptoms of shock include the following:

Sweaty but cool (clammy) skin.

Pale skin color.

Blotchy or bluish skin, especially around the mouth.

Rapid or severe bleeding.

Nausea/vomiting.

Anxiety. (Anxiety causes the heart to beat faster, thus increasing the rate of blood circulation and the rate of blood loss. Anxiety can increase as the casualty's condition worsens. He may become restless, agitated, and may even become violent and fight the people around them.)

Mental confusion. (Mental confusion is especially dangerous because the casualty may not comprehend their surroundings and may expose themself and others to danger needlessly.)

Increased breathing rate.

Unusual thirst.

3.   POSITION   THE   CASUALTY   TO PREVENT/CONTROL SHOCK

Shock is a life-threatening condition. Once you have ensured that the casualty is breathing and have controlled any major bleeding, dressed any major wounds, and splinted any major fractures, you must take measures to prevent shock if it is not present or to control shock if it is present. The procedures for preventing shock are the same as the procedures for controlling (treating) shock.

Normal Shock Position

Most casualties should be placed in the normal shock position described below.

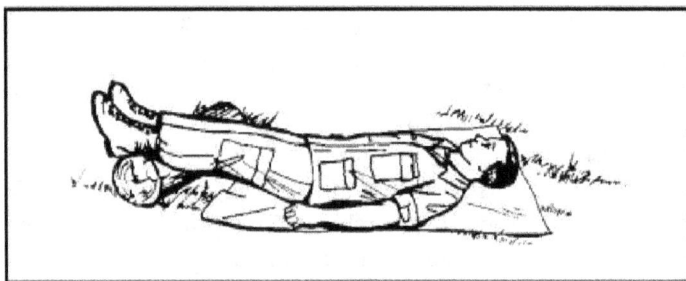

NORMAL POSITIONING OF CASUALTY TO
CONTROL SHOCK

Move the casualty to cover if it is available and the situation permits.

Position the casualty on their back. If possible, place a poncho or blanket under the casualty to protect them from the temperature or dampness of the ground.

Elevate the casualty's legs so that their feet are slightly higher than the level of their heart. (This helps the blood in the veins of their legs to return to their heart.)

WARNING
Do not elevate the legs until all fractures have been splinted.

Place a small log, field pack, box, rolled field jacket, or other stable object under the casualty's feet or ankles in order to maintain the elevation.

Shock Positions for Special Injuries

Certain casualties are not placed in the normal position for shock. Proper positioning of casualties with special injuries is discussed below.

Suspected Fracture of the Spine. Do not move a casualty with a suspected spinal fracture. Do not elevate their legs. Immobilize their head, neck, and back if possible.

Open Abdominal Wound. Place the casualty on their back with their knees flexed.

Open Chest Wound. If the casualty wishes to sit up, help them to sit. If possible, have them sit with their back to a wall, tree, or other support. If the casualty wishes to lie down, position them so that he is lying on their injured side.

Heart Attack. Allow the casualty to sit up with their back to a wall or other support if he wants to do so. Otherwise, position the casualty on their side.

Head Wound. Treat a major head wound as though a spinal injury is present. A casualty with a minor head wound should be allowed to sit up if there is no bleeding into the mouth. If the casualty has bleeding into the mouth or if he does not want to sit up, position them on their side with their head turned so that the blood can drain from their mouth. Position them with their wound up.

Unconsciousness. Position an unconscious casualty on their side with their head turned so that any fluids can drain from their mouth. If the casualty vomits, perform a finger sweep to clear their airway before he can inhale the vomitus.

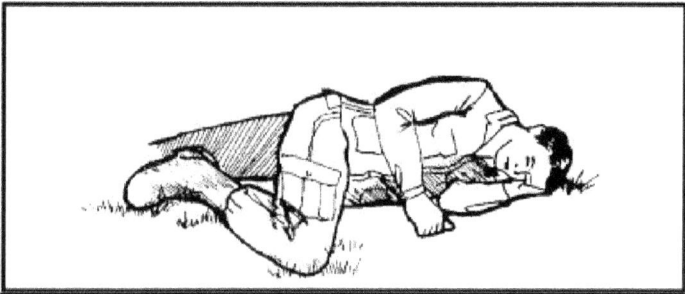

UNCONSCIOUS CASUALTY POSITIONED ON
THEIR SIDE

4.   TAKE   ADDITIONAL   MEASURES   TO
PREVENT/CONTROL SHOCK

Additional actions for preventing or controlling
hypovolemic shock are given below.

Reassure the Casualty

Keep the casualty calm. Tell the casualty that you
are helping them. Be confident in your ability to help the
casualty and have a "take charge" attitude. Your words and
actions can do much to reassure the casualty and reduce
their anxiety. Be careful of any comments that you make
regarding the casualty's condition since unguarded
comments could increase the casualty's anxiety.

Loosen the Casualty's Clothing

Loosen the casualty's clothing at their neck, waist,
feet, or anywhere that it may be binding. Tight clothing can
interfere with blood circulation.

Keep the Casualty From Being Too Warm or Too Cool

In warm weather, keep the casualty in the shade. If
natural shade is not available, erect an improvised shade
using a poncho and sticks or other available materials. Fan
them if needed.   (Fanning promotes the evaporation of
perspiration and cools the casualty.)

In cool weather, cover the casualty with a blanket,
poncho, or other available materials to keep them warm and
dry. Place cover under the casualty to prevent chilling due
to contact with cold or wet ground.   (Note: Dress and
bandage any serious burns before covering them.)

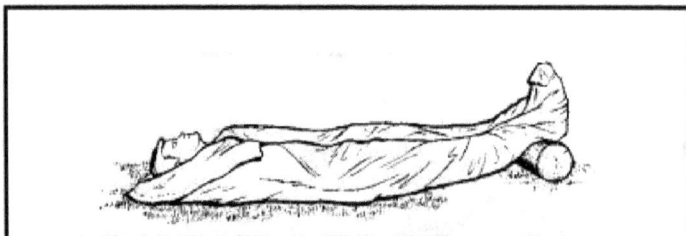

CASUALTY BEING TREATED FOR SHOCK IN COOL
WEATHER

If you must leave a casualty for any reason (casualty
cannot be moved due to a spinal injury, for example),
reassure the casualty by telling them that you will return.
Turn the casualty's head to one side before you leave. This

186

will help to keep the casualty from choking on their own vomitus should he vomit. Do **not** give the casualty food or water.

FIRST AID FOR A SUSPECTED FRACTURE

1. INTRODUCTION

A fracture is a break in a bone. A fracture can cause discomfort, disability, and even death.

A closed fracture is a break in the bone without a break in the skin. Even

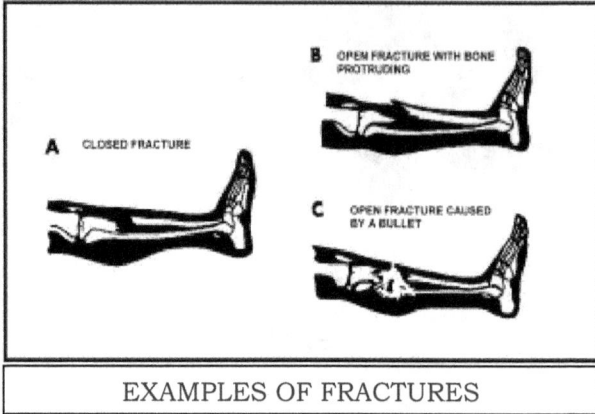

A CLOSED FRACTURE

B OPEN FRACTURE WITH BONE PROTRUDING

C OPEN FRACTURE CAUSED BY A BULLET

EXAMPLES OF FRACTURES

though the skin is not cut or broken, the tissue beneath the skin may be damaged.

An open fracture is a break in the bone with a break in the overlying skin as well. The break in the skin may be caused by the sharp end of the broken bone or by a foreign object such as a bullet penetrating the skin. Open fractures are especially serious due to the danger of infection.

A dislocation occurs when the bones comprising a joint (elbow, knee, wrist, etc.) are forced out of their proper positions. A sprain results when a joint is twisted beyond its normal limits of motion and the connecting tissues around the joint tear. A dislocation or sprain can produce signs and symptoms similar to those of a fracture and should be treated as a fracture of the joint.

3. IDENTIFY SIGNS AND SYMPTOMS OF A FRACTURED SPINE

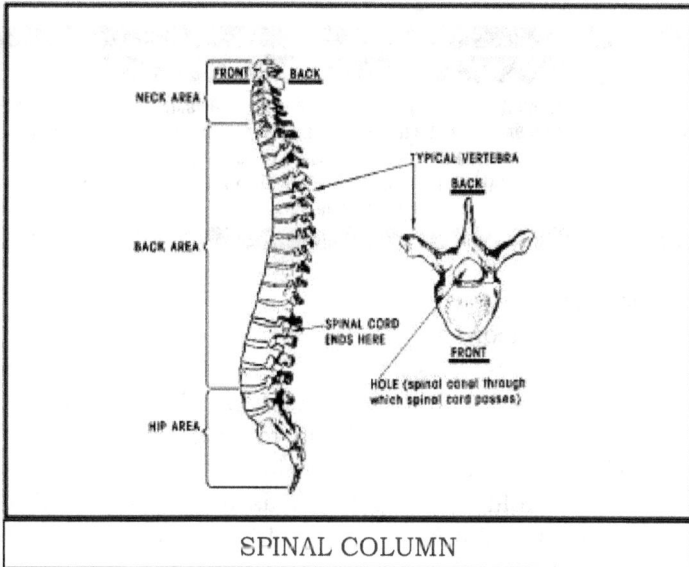

FRONT ← **BACK**
NECK AREA
TYPICAL VERTEBRA
BACK
BACK AREA
SPINAL CORD ENDS HERE
FRONT
HIP AREA
HOLE (spinal canal through which spinal cord passes)

SPINAL COLUMN

The spinal column (also called the backbone or spine) consists of a series of bones called vertebrae. The top seven vertebrae are the bones of the neck. The spinal column surrounds and protects the spinal cord. The spinal cord consists of nerves which carry impulses between the brain and the rest of the body. If the spinal cord is severed (cut completely), the muscles controlled by the portion of the spinal cord below the cut will not function. Always check for a spinal injury if the casualty has suffered a fall or has been hit in the back.

Signs and symptoms of an injured spine include:

Pain or tenderness of the neck or back.

Cut or bruise on the neck or back.

Inability to move part of the body (paralysis), especially the legs.

Lack of feeling in a body part. (Touch the casualty's arms and legs and ask if he feels your hand.)

Loss of bladder and/or bowel control.

Head or back in an unusual position.

3. IMMOBILIZE A FRACTURED SPINE

189

Treat any casualty which you think may have a spinal injury as though you were certain that he had a fractured spine.

Tell the casualty to keep still. Any movement could cause additional injury.

Send someone to get medical help.

If the casualty is lying on their stomach, keep them from moving until medical help arrives. If the casualty is lying on their back, use padding to help immobilize their back, neck, and head as described in the following pages.

Roll or fold padding (such as a blanket) so that it conforms to the shape of the arch of their back. Then carefully slide the padding under the arch of their back. This padding will help to support and immobilize their back.

Slide a roll of cloth under the casualty's neck to help support and immobilize their neck.

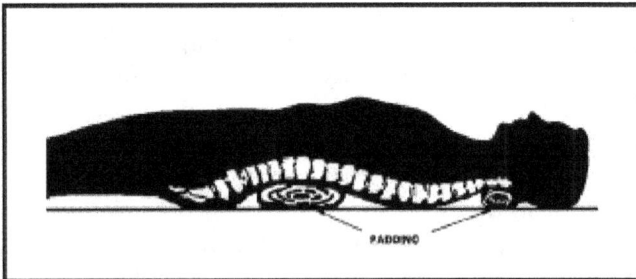

PADDING PLACED UNDER BACK AND NECK

Place padded rocks, small padded logs, or filled boots on each side of the casualty's head to keep it from moving.

IMMOBILIZING THE HEAD WITH BOOTS

To prepare filled boots:

Remove the casualty's boots.

Fill the boots almost to the top with sand or small rocks.

Place material (strip of clothing, sock, etc.) on top of the sand or rocks to keep the sand or rocks from falling out.

Tie the top of the boots to keep the material from coming out.

Place the boots around the casualty's head.

4. IDENTIFY SIGNS AND SYMPTOMS OF A FRACTURED ARM OR LEG

Some of the signs and symptoms of a fractured arm or leg are given below.

Bone sticking through the skin.

Feeling what appears to be a break in the bone.

Pain, tenderness, swelling, and/or bruises at a particular location. (The site of the tenderness or bruise is probably the site of the fracture.)

Arm or leg in an abnormal position (looks deformed).

Difficulty in moving an arm or leg. (NOTE: Do not have the casualty attempt to move the injured arm or leg to test this symptom. Rely upon what the casualty tells you.)

Massive injury to an arm or leg. (Even if the arm or leg is not broken, the pain caused by the wound may be lessened if the arm or leg is splinted after it has been dressed and bandaged.)

"Snapping" sound heard by the casualty at the time of the injury.

5. PREPARE THE CASUALTY PRIOR TO SPLINTING

Once you have located the site of the fracture, you must splint the injured arm or leg. (A splint is a rigid object or objects secured to the injured limb so as to prevent the broken bone from moving. If the fractured bone is not splinted, the sharp end of the broken bone could move and injure surrounding muscles, blood vessels, and nerves.) Before applying the splint, however, you should prepare the casualty.

Reassure Casualty

Tell the casualty that you are taking care of them. If you must leave the casualty to locate a rigid object or securing materials, be sure to tell them that you will return quickly. Talk to the casualty even if he appears to be unconscious.

Loosen Clothing

Loosen any clothing that is tight or which binds the casualty. Boots should not be removed unless they are needed to immobilize an injured neck or there is bleeding from the foot.

Remove Jewelry

Remove any jewelry that is on the casualty's injured limb and put the jewelry into their pocket. Jewelry is removed because the limb may swell and cause the jewelry to interfere with blood circulation. Be sure to tell the casualty what you are doing and why.

Check Circulation Below Fracture

Evaluate the casualty's blood circulation in the limb below the fracture site. Poor circulation can lead to the loss of the limb if left untreated.

Numbness. If the area feels numb or tingling to the casualty, the area probably has poor circulation.

Color. In a light-skinned person, a pale, white, or bluish-gray skin color indicates poor circulation. To check the circulation in a dark-skinned individual, press on a nail on the injured limb and the corresponding nail on the uninjured arm or leg. Release both nails at the same time. If the color returns to the nail bed of the uninjured limb faster than it returns to the nail bed of the injured limb, the casualty probably has poor circulation in the injured limb.

Temperature. Place your hand on the area beneath the injury. Then place your hand on the corresponding area on the uninjured arm or leg. If the skin of the injured limb is cooler that the skin on the uninjured limb, the casualty probably has poor circulation in the injured limb.

Dress Wounds

Dress any open wounds on the injured limb before applying the splint. If a bone is sticking out, do not attempt to push the bone back under the skin. Apply the dressing over the bone and the wound. Do not attempt to straighten or realign the injured limb.

6. PREPARE THE SPLINT

Gather Materials

Gather the materials you will need to make the splint. You will need something to use as the rigid object, padding, and securing material to keep the splint from slipping.

Rigid Object. Tree branches, poles, boards, sticks, unloaded rifles, or other rigid objects can be used. Normally, two rigid objects (one for each side of the limb) are used. The rigid objects should be fairly straight and be long enough to extend beyond the joint above the fracture site and beyond the joint below the fracture site. Even the casualty's own body can be used when other materials are not available. Their chest can be used to immobilize a fractured arm and an uninjured leg can be used to immobilize a fractured leg.

Padding. Blankets, jackets, ponchos, extra clothing, shelter halves, or leafy plants can be used to pad the splint. In some cases, you may have to use the casualty's trouser leg or shirt sleeve as padding. Padding is necessary to keep the rigid object from rubbing against the skin on the injured limb.

Securing Materials. Rigid objects can be secured with strips of clothing, belts, pistol belts, bandoleers, cravats, or similar materials. Cravats are preferred when possible. Narrow materials such as wire and cord should not be used to secure the rigid object in place since they could interfere with blood circulation. The steps for making cravats are summarized below.

Cut or tear a square about three feet on each side from pliable material such as a shirt or sheet.

Fold the square along the diagonal so that it is triangular in shape.

Cut or tear along the fold so that two triangles are formed. (Each triangle becomes a cravat.)

Fold top of the triangle down until the tip of the triangle touches the base (longest side).

Continue to fold until the cravat is of the correct size.

Position the Rigid Objects

Place the rigid objects so that one is on each side of the injured limb. When possible, position the rigid objects so that the joint above the fracture and the joint below the fracture can be immobilized. If the fracture is in the lower leg, for example, the splint should extend above the knee and below the ankle. (Note: If a forearm is fractured, the wrist is usually immobilized by the splint and the elbow is usually immobilized by a sling and swathe.) Make sure that the ends of the rigid objects are not pressing against a sensitive area such as the armpit or groin. Pressure on these areas can interfere with blood circulation.

Apply Padding

Place padding between the rigid objects and the body part to be splinted. The padding helps to prevent excessive pressure on the limb which could interfere with blood circulation. Extra padding should be used at bony body areas such as the elbow, wrist, knee, or ankle and extra-sensitive areas such as the groin and armpit.

7. APPLY THE SPLINT

Position the securing materials. Push the securing material (cravat, etc.) under natural body curvatures, such as the knee. Then gently move the securing material up or down the limb until the material is in proper position.

CAUTION
Do not place securing material directly under the suspected fracture site. The pressure caused by the securing material when it is tightened could cause additional injury to the fracture site.

Place securing material under the limb both above and below the fracture site. If possible, place two cravats above the fracture site and two cravats below the fracture site (above the upper joint, between the upper joint and the fracture, between the fracture and the lower joint, and below the lower joint.)

Place the padded rigid objects on the securing materials and against the injured limb.

Wrap the securing materials around the rigid objects and limb so that the rigid objects immobilize the limb. Tie the ends (tails) of each securing cravat in a nonslip knot on the outer rigid object and away from the casualty. (The knots are tied on the outer rather than the inner rigid object

WARNING
Do not try to straighten or reposition the fractured limb. Splint the limb in the position you find it. Move the limb as little as possible while applying and securing the splint.

to make loosening and retying the cravats easier should that procedure become necessary.) The securing material should be tight enough to hold the rigid objects securely in place, but not tight enough to interfere with blood circulation.

Observe the limb below the cravats for signs of impaired circulation as you secure the splints. After the splint has been secured, recheck the limb's circulation to ensure that the cravats or rigid objects have not interfered with blood circulation. Check the color and temperature of the limb and ask the casualty how the limb feels. If your check before splinting the fracture showed normal circulation and your check now shows poor circulation (bluish skin, slow return of color to nail bed, coolness, or a numb or tingling sensation in the limb), take the following measures to restore circulation.

Loosen the securing strips/cravats.

If the end of the rigid object is pressing against the casualty's body (especially under the arm or inside the thigh), reposition the rigid object and/or add padding.

Retie the securing materials using nonslip knots on the outer rigid object. Make sure that the securing materials keep the rigid objects from slipping, but are not tight enough to interfere with blood circulation.

Recheck the circulation.

8. APPLY A SLING TO A FRACTURED ARM

A sling can be used to support an injured arm with a fractured forearm, wrist, or hand. When the upper arm is fractured, a sling can be used to help immobilize the forearm and elbow. Apply and secure padded rigid objects to immobilize the fracture before applying the sling. (NOTE: If the chest is to be used as the rigid object, apply the sling before securing the upper arm to the chest with swathes.)

A sling can be made using a triangular bandage, strips of torn material, or the casualty's shirt or jacket.

Triangular Bandage Sling

A triangular bandage sling can be made from any available non-stretching material such as a muslin bandage, fatigue shirt, trousers, poncho, blanket, or shelter-half.

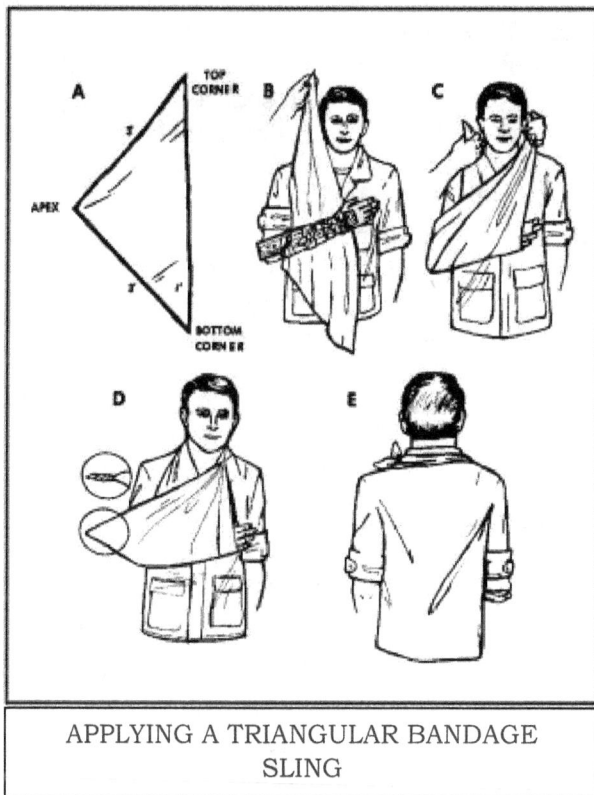

APPLYING A TRIANGULAR BANDAGE
SLING

Cut or tear the material into a triangular shape (same as making a cravat).

Insert the material under the injured arm so that the arm is in the center of the material, the apex of the sling is beyond the elbow, and the top corner of the material is over the shoulder of the injured side.

Position the forearm so that the hand is slightly higher than the elbow (at about a 10 degree angle).

Bring the lower portion of the material over the injured arm so that the bottom corner goes over the shoulder of the uninjured side.

Bring the top corner behind the casualty's neck.

Tie the two corners together so that the knot will not slip. The knot should fit into the "hollow" at the side of the neck on the uninjured side. (If the right arm is fractured, for example, tie the knot so that it will rest in the hollow on the left side of their neck.)

Twist the apex of the sling and tuck it in at the elbow. (The corner can also be secured using a safety pin.) This secures the elbow and keeps the forearm from slipping out of the sling.

Jacket Flap Sling

Position the forearm on the casualty's chest with the hand positioned slightly higher than the elbow.

Undo the jacket so that the lower portion (flap) can be brought over the arm to form a sling.

Bring the flap up over the forearm to the pocket area. Position the elbow so that it is inside the sling and will not slip out of the sling.

Push a stick or other rigid object through the flap

JACKET FLAP SLING

and the upper portion of the jacket so the flap will not slip.

9. APPLY A SWATHE TO A FRACTURED ARM

A swathe is a band or wrapping used to further immobilize an arm once the fracture has been splinted. A large strip of cloth, blanket strip, pistol belt, trouser belt, bandoleer, or other material can be used as a swathe. The swathe should be three to six inches wide.

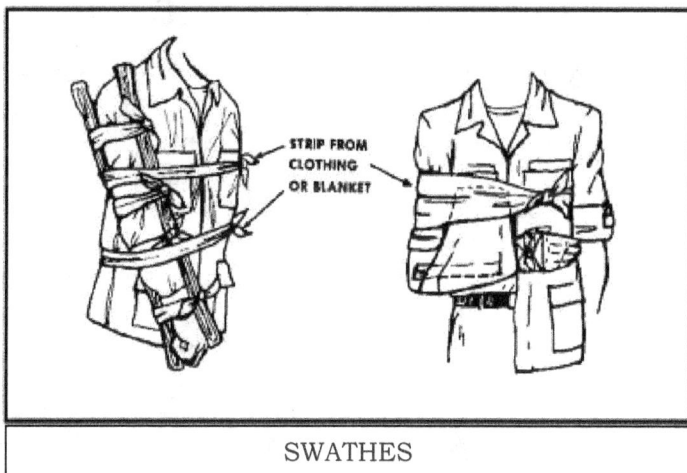

SWATHES

Place one end of the swathe at the breast pocket nearest the uninjured arm.

Wrap the swathe across the sling (if used), around the upper arm on the injured side, behind the casualty's back, <u>under</u> the uninjured arm, and back to the breast pocket.

Tie the two ends in a nonslip knot.

When possible, apply two swathes.

When swathes are used to immobilize a splinted arm without a sling, a swathe is applied above the fracture site and another swathe is applied below the fracture site.

CAUTION
**Do not apply a swathe on top of the fracture site.
The pressure of the swathe could cause additional damage to the nerves and blood vessels around the broken bone.**

FIRST AID FOR A HEAT INJURY

1. INTRODUCTION

Heat injuries usually occur during hot weather or when a person is working near equipment that produces heat. The body perspires in order to cool itself. If the water and the salt lost through perspiration are not adequately replaced, heat injuries can result. Even a healthy person can suffer heat injury. Heat injuries can be painful and, in some cases, fatal. The three principal types of heat injuries are heat cramps, heat exhaustion, and heatstroke.

2. IDENTIFY SIGNS AND SYMPTOMS OF HEAT CRAMPS

Heat cramps are painful muscle spasms (contractions) caused by loss of water and salt from the body, usually through perspiration. Signs and symptoms of heat cramps include:

Grasping or massaging an arm or leg.

Bending over in an effort to relieve the pain of an abdominal cramp.

Skin wet with perspiration.

Unusual thirst.

3. IDENTIFY SIGNS AND SYMPTOMS OF HEAT EXHAUSTION

Heat exhaustion is more serious than heat cramps. It is primarily caused by the body losing water, usually through perspiration, without the water being adequately replaced. Heat exhaustion usually occurs in otherwise fit individuals who are involved in extreme physical exertion in a hot environment. The signs and symptoms of heat exhaustion are very similar to those of shock. The signs and symptoms can be divided into two groups-the most common signs and symptoms and those which are less likely to occur.

- Common Signs and Symptoms of Heat Exhaustion
- Profuse sweating with pale, moist, cool skin.
- Weakness or faintness.
- Dizziness.
- Headache.

- Loss of appetite.
- Other Signs and Symptoms of Heat Exhaustion
- Heat cramps.
- Nausea (with or without vomiting).
- Chills ("gooseflesh").
- Rapid breathing.
- Urge to defecate.
- Tingling in hands or feet.
- Mental confusion.

4.   IDENTIFY SIGNS AND SYMPTOMS OF HEATSTROKE

Heatstroke (also called sunstroke) usually occurs in people who work in a very hot, humid environment for a prolonged period of time. In heatstroke, the body's cooling mechanisms (perspiration, etc.) fail and the body's internal (core) temperature increases to dangerous levels. If the casualty's body temperature is not lowered quickly, death may result. The following are signs and symptoms of heatstroke.

- Lack of normal perspiration.
- Skin that is hot and flushed.
- Headache.
- Dizziness.
- Mental confusion.
- Stomach pains.
- Weakness.
- Nausea.
- Seizures.
- Rapid breathing.
- Sudden loss of consciousness.

WARNING

A person who is not perspiring or perspiring very little while other soldiers performing the same work are perspiring freely is in danger of being a heatstroke casualty. Take buddy-aid measures immediately.

5. TREAT HEAT CRAMPS

Move the casualty to a cool shaded area to rest. If there is no shade, improvise a shade using ponchos, blankets, or other available materials.

Loosen the casualty's clothing around their neck and waist and loosen their boots.

Have the casualty slowly drink one quart (one canteen) of cool water. (Drinking the water too rapidly may cause the casualty to vomit, thus losing even more fluids.)

6. TREAT HEAT EXHAUSTION

Move the casualty to a cool shaded area to rest. If there is no shade, improvise a shade using ponchos, blankets, or other available materials.

Have the casualty lie on their back.

Loosen or remove the casualty's clothing around their neck and waist and loosen their boots.

Pour water over the casualty and fan them in order to cool their body faster.

Have the casualty slowly drink at least a canteen (one quart) of cool water.

Elevate the casualty's feet above the level of their heart (put a log or other supporting object under their feet or ankles).

Monitor the casualty. When possible, seek medical aid.

If possible, the casualty should not participate in strenuous activity for the remainder of the day.

7. TREAT HEATSTROKE

Heatstroke is a **medical emergency**. The casualty could die if he is not treated in time. If possible, send someone to get medical help while you work with the casualty. Move the casualty to a cool, shaded area or improvise a shade.

Have the casualty lie down and elevate their legs.

Loosen or remove the casualty's outer garments.

The preferred method is to spray or pour cool water over the casualty. Fan the casualty to increase the rate of evaporation and thus cool the casualty faster. Massage the casualty's arms and legs with cool water. Massaging their arms and legs help to increase the blood circulation in their limbs. Increased blood circulation will result in the body being able to give off more heat, thus cooling the body.

Have the casualty slowly drink one quart of cool water if he is able. Monitor the casualty's breathing. Administer Rescue Breathing if needed.

Patrick J Shrier
FIRST AID FOR COLD INJURIES

1. Cold injuries are most likely to occur when an unprepared individual is exposed to winter temperatures. The cold weather and the type of activity in which the individual is involved impact on whether he or she is likely to be injured and to what extent. Clothing, physical condition, and mental makeup also are determining factors. However, cold injuries can usually be prevented. Well-disciplined and well-trained individuals can be protected even in the most adverse circumstances. The extent of the cold injury depends upon duration of exposure and adequacy of protection. Individuals with a history of cold injury are more likely to suffer cold injuries. The body parts most easily affected by cold are the cheeks, nose, ears, chin, forehead, wrists, hands, and feet. Proper treatment and management depend upon accurate diagnosis.

2. IDENTIFY SIGNS AND SYMPTOMS OF **CHILBLAIN/FROSTNIP**

Chilblain is caused by repeated prolonged exposure of bare skin at temperature from 60°F to 32°F, or 20°F for acclimated, dry, unwashed skin. Signs and symptoms are the following:

- Redness or pallor of affected areas (fingers, nose, ears).
- Hot, tender, itching skin.
- Absence of pain (numb).
- May have ulcerated or bleeding lesions.

3. IDENTIFY SIGNS AND SYMPTOMS OF **FROSTBITE**

Frostbite is the injury of tissue caused from exposure to cold, usually below 32° F depending on the wind-chill factor, duration of exposure, and adequacy of protection. Frostbite usually occurs in the cheeks, nose, ears, chin, forehead, fingers, hands, wrists, toes, or feet. These areas are more likely to be exposed to cold conditions. These areas also have poorer blood circulation than other parts of the body, and blood carries warmth as well as nutrients.

Superficial frostbite

204

Superficial frostbite primarily involves injury to the skin and the tissue just beneath the skin. Signs and symptoms of superficial frostbite, listed in the order in which they would appear with increased exposure and time, include:

- A tingling sensation, followed by numbness.
- A sudden blanching (whitening) of the affected area.
- A reddish (in light-skinned individuals) or grayish (in dark-skinned individuals) area on the skin. If the temperature is above freezing, this condition is called chilblain.

Deep frostbite

Deep frostbite occurs when the tissues below the skin freeze. This may include the tissues of the muscles and bones. The blanching and numbness of superficial frostbite always precede the development of deep frostbite. If not properly treated, frostbite can result in the loss of fingers, toes, hands, or feet. It can also result in gangrene – a life-threatening condition. Signs and symptoms of deep frostbite include:

- Blisters and sloughing (flaking in large sheets) of affected skin (may occur 24 to 36 hours after exposure).
- Swelling or tender areas.
- Loss of previous feeling of pain in the affected area.
- Pale, yellowish, waxy-looking skin.
- Frozen area feels solid or wooden to the touch.

The above frostbite signs and symptoms are applicable to the face, hands, and feet. Deep frostbite is a very serious injury that requires immediate First Aid and subsequent medical treatment to avoid or minimize loss of body parts.

4. IDENTIFY SIGNS AND SYMPTOMS OF **IMMERSION FOOT/TRENCH FOOT**

Immersion foot and trench foot are injuries that result from fairly long exposure of the feet to wet conditions at temperatures from approximately 50°F to 32°F. Inactive feet in damp or wet socks and boots or tightly laced boots which impair circulation are even more susceptible to injury. Signs and symptoms are as follows:

- Early stages/first phase of immersion foot
- The affected area feels cold.
- The affected area feels numb and painless.
- The pulse is diminished/absent in the affected area.
- Later stages/advanced immersion foot
- The limbs feel hot and burning.
- There are shooting pains in the affected area.
- The affected area is pale with a bluish cast.
- The pulse strength is decreased.
- Some other signs that may follow are: blisters, swelling, redness, heat hemorrhages, and gangrene.

5. IDENTIFY SIGNS AND SYMPTOMS OF **SNOWBLINDNESS**

Snow blindness is the effect that glare from an ice field or snow field has on the eyes. It is more likely to occur in hazy, cloudy weather than when the sun is shining. Glare from the sun will normally cause an individual to instinctively protect their eyes. Signs and symptoms are as follows:

- Scratchy feeling in the eyes, as if from sand or dirt.
- Watery eyes.
- Redness in the eyes.
- The casualty may have a headache.
- Increased pain with exposure to light.

6. IDENTIFY SIGNS AND SYMPTOMS OF **HYPOTHERMIA**

The destructive influence of cold on the body is called hypothermia (general cooling). This means the body loses heat faster than it can produce it. Hypothermia and frostbite may occur at the same time with exposure to below-freezing temperatures. Hypothermia may occur from exposure to temperatures above freezing, especially from immersion in cold water, wet-cold conditions, or from the effect of wind. Physical exhaustion and insufficient food intake may also increase the risk of hypothermia. Signs

> ## **WARNING**
> **With generalized hypothermia, the entire body has cooled with the core temperature below 95°F/35°C. THIS IS A MEDICAL EMERGENCY.**

and symptoms are given below.

Mild hypothermia (body temperature 90°to 95°F/32°to 35°C).

(**NOTE:** Reference to temperatures is made to give you an idea of what is taking place in the body of the casualty.)

Hypothermia should be suspected in any chronically ill person who is found in an environment of less than 50°F/10°C.

- The casualty is conscious, but usually apathetic or lethargic.
- The casualty is shivering.
- The skin is pale, cold.
- The casualty speaks with slurred speech.
- The casualty has poor muscle coordination.
- There is a faint pulse.

Severe hypothermia (body temperature 90°F/32°C or lower).

- The casualty's breathing is slow and shallow.
- There is irregular heart action.
- The pulse is weaker or even absent.
- The casualty appears to be in a stupor or is unconscious.
- The skin is ice cold.
- The casualty's muscles are rigid.
- The eyes are glassy.

7.   IDENTIFY SIGNS AND SYMPTOMS OF **DEHYDRATION (COLD WEATHER)**

Dehydration (cold weather) occurs when the body loses too much fluid, salt, and minerals. When individuals engage in any strenuous exercises or activities, an excessive amount of fluid and salt is lost through sweat. The danger of dehydration is that it is as prevalent in cold regions as it is in hot regions. In cold weather, it is extremely difficult to realize that this condition exists. Signs and symptoms the casualty may exhibit are given below.

- The mouth, tongue, and throat are parched and dry.
- Swallowing is difficult.
- Nausea and dizziness may be present.
- The casualty may faint.
- There is a feeling of being tired and weak.
- There may be muscle cramps, especially in the legs.
- The casualty may have difficulty focusing their eyes.

8. TREAT CHILBLAIN/FROSTNIP

Chilblain is treated by warming the injured body part. Blow warm air on the part or place the body part in contact with a warm object, such as a caregiver's hands or the casualty's body. If the hands are affected, the casualty can cross their arms and place their hands under their armpits.

Once the body part is rewarmed, protect it from further cold exposure.

9. TREAT FROSTBITE

Frostbite is treated by rewarming the affected area slowly and protecting the affected area from refreezing. Move the casualty to the most protected area available and perform the following warming procedures.

(**NOTE**: These rewarming procedures can also be used to treat yourself if you begin to develop a cold injury.)

Face

Cover the frostbitten area on the casualty's face with your bare hands. Leave your hands in place until the pain in the frostbitten area stops and the color returns to the area.

Cover the casualty with blankets or other dry material to keep them warm and to avoid additional injuries from the cold. Give them warm, nonalcoholic liquids to drink, if available.

Hand

Remove jewelry from the affected hand and put it in the casualty's pocket. Loosen constricting clothing to help restore circulation.

Open the casualty's field jacket and shirt.

Place the casualty's frostbitten hand(s) under the armpits (right hand under left armpit; left hand under right armpit).

Close the casualty's clothing to prevent additional exposure to the cold.

Cover the casualty with blankets or other dry material to keep them warm and to avoid additional injuries from the cold.

Give the casualty warm, nonalcoholic liquids to drink, if available.

Feet

Loosen constricting clothing to help restore circulation.

Remove the boot and sock from the frostbitten foot.

Have another soldier (yourself if no other soldier is available) undo their clothing so that the casualty's foot (or feet) can be placed next to the soldier's abdomen.

Place the casualty's frostbitten foot (or feet) against the abdomen of the second soldier.

Close the second soldier's clothing as much as possible in order to provide additional warmth to the foot (feet) and to protect the second soldier's body from the cold.

Cover the casualty with blankets or other dry material to keep them warm and to avoid additional injuries from the cold.

Give them warm, nonalcoholic liquids to drink, if available.

The casualty should exercise as much as possible while avoiding trauma to the injured part.

Actions to avoid in treating frostbite.

A well-meaning person can perform certain procedures which can result in harming the person he is trying to help. You should be familiar with these rules.

Snow. Do not rub the frostbitten area with snow or ice. Snow or ice will increase heat loss.

Soaking. Do not soak the frostbitten area. Hot or cold soaks can damage tissue.

Extreme Heat. Do not expose the frostbitten area to extreme heat, such as a fire. Burns can result since the casualty will not be able to judge heat accurately.

Massaging. Do not rub or massage the frostbitten area. Manipulation can cause damage to the tissue.

Alcohol. Do not give the casualty alcoholic beverages. Alcohol causes the blood vessels near the surface to enlarge which results in heat loss.

Tobacco. Do not give the casualty tobacco products. Tobacco promotes heat loss.

Ointments. Do not apply ointment to the affected area. The moisture in the ointment can freeze and cause additional damage to the affected area.

10. TREAT IMMERSION FOOT/TRENCH FOOT

Gradually rewarm by exposing to warm air. Do not apply heat or ice. Do not moisten or massage the foot.

Protect affected parts from trauma.

Dry the feet thoroughly and avoid walking.

Elevate the affected part.

11. TREAT SNOW BLINDNESS

Cover the casualty's eyes with a dark cloth.

12. TREAT FOR HYPOTHERMIA.

Mild hypothermia.

Rewarm the body evenly using a heat source such as a campfire or another soldier's body. Merely placing the casualty in a sleeping bag or covering with a blanket is not enough since the casualty is unable to generate sufficient body heat on their own.

Keep the casualty dry and protected from the elements.

Have a conscious casualty drink warm liquids gradually.

Seek medical treatment immediately.

Severe hypothermia.

CAUTION

Rewarming a severely hypothermic casualty is extremely dangerous in the field due to the great possibility of such complications as rewarming shock and disturbance in the rhythm of the heartbeat.

Stabilize the temperature by using heat sources such as: camp fire, electric blankets, hot water bottle, etc. The object is to warm the body evenly and quickly.

Attempt to avoid further heat loss by using blankets, sleeping bags, etc. Remove wet clothing before covering the soldier with blankets or using a sleeping bag. Move the casualty to a place of warmth, if possible.

13. TREAT DEHYDRATION (COLD WEATHER)

Keep the casualty warm.

Loosen the casualty's clothes to improve circulation.

Give the casualty fluids for fluid replacement.

Have the casualty rest.

CHAPTER 8 – USEFUL AND HELPFUL KNOTS

"We learn the rope of life by untying its knots."

Jean Toomer (20th Century American Poet & Novelist of the Harlem Rennaissance)

There are many more knots out there than the ones in this book. I have chosen the ones that I consider both the most useful and the easiest for a novice to tie.

All of the knots I discuss can be tied with just about any rope or twine but I prefer 550 Cord, the most useful rope/cord ever invented. A useful thing to do with all the 550 Cord you have is to take a lighter and slightly melt the ends and let it cool off to seal the end of the cord and stop the interior cords from retracting.

I highly encourage anyone who wants to learn more knots to take the time to research and learn them before the balloon goes up and you find yourself alone in the woods trying to figure out how to cross a 50-foot ravine. There are a couple of terms used when talking about knots that are useful to know or else it is difficult to understand what the instructions really mean.

- Bend: A knot for joining two knots together
- Bight: Generally this means an arc in the rope that makes a semicircle; it can also mean just the part in between the standing and working ends of the rope.
- Hitch: A knot used to attach a rope to an object such as a ring, post, or another rope
- Lashing: A knot used to two or more objects together rigidly
- Loop: A section of the bight that makes a circle and crosses over itself
- Sinnet: A braid used to store ropes by shortening the overall length of the rope or cord
- Standing End: The standing end of a rope is the part not active in knot tying (i.e. just lying there passively)
- Whipping: A binding tied around the end of a rope to keep it from unraveling
- Working End: The working end of a rope is the part that is active in knot tying (i.e. the end of the rope manipulated)

Some additional sources of information on the bewildering variety of knots can be found at: the English Wikipedia (https://en.wikipedia.org/wiki/List_of_knots),

Survivalworld's Knots page. (http://survivalworld.com/knots/#.UiLm_RscZsI), and netknots.com (http://www.netknots.com/). There are many other web resources on knots as well although I have found the three listed here to be the most useful and clear.

HALF HITCH

The Half Hitch is one of the basic knots that everybody should know. In concept it is essentially a single hitch formed around the standing part of another hitch. The main use of the half-hitch is to complete and strengthen other knots so that they do not unravel.

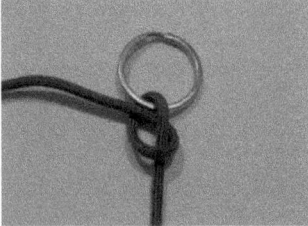

A Single Half Hitch is formed by taking the working end through a ring or around an object, back out over the standing part, and through the loop. Pull on the working end and the standing part to tighten.

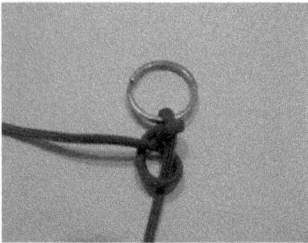

1.   To form Two Half Hitches take the working end around again, over the standing part and through the loop.

2.   The Slipped Half Hitch is formed by placing a bight between the loop and the standing part; one sharp pull on the working end releases the knot.

CLOVE HITCH

A Clove Hitch is simply two successive half-hitches tied around an object. It is used to secure a rope to a standing object and can also be used to tie two or more objects together making a lashing. Tying a Clove-Hitch is a simple 3 step process:

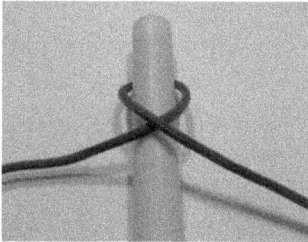

1.   Wrap the free end of your rope or cord around the object or objects to be tied together.

2.   Cross the rope over itself and back around the object.

3.   Slip the working end under the second wrap & pull the knot tight.

CHAIN SINNET

A chain sinnet is a very useful knot for storing cord or rope. It reduces the length of the cord by about 2/3 and can be untied by simply untying the locking knot and pulling on the cord. This knot can also be used to store cord by wrapping the rope or cord around objects or loops of itself. I use the heck out of this knot to store not only lengths of plain 550 Cord, I also wrap the frame of my rucksack with additional 550 Cord. I am a firm believer that you can never have enough 550 Cord because just when you think you don't need it you most assuredly will.

Tying the sinnet is very easy and with practice you can tie it without really even thinking about it. To tie a Chain Sinnet:

1. Create a loop in the rope. Then pull a bight of the working part through the loop, creating an overhand noose knot.

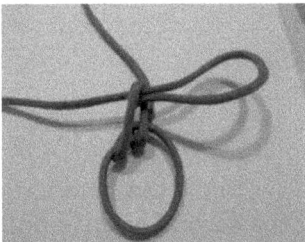

2. Pull another bight of the working part through the loop of the previous stitch.

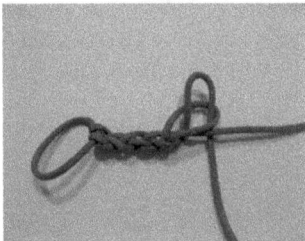

3. Tighten the stitch to the desired degree by pulling on both sides of the loop. Adjust the loop by pulling on the working end to keep it a reasonable size.

The Simple Survival Smart Book

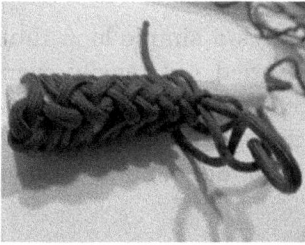

4. Repeat steps 2-3 until there is approximately 8 inches of rope left.

5.

6. To lock the sinnet, pass the working end through the final loop.

6.   To restore the rope to its original length, pull the end passed in the last step back through the final loop and pull on the free end. The sinnet will quickly unravel.

BOWLINE KNOT

The Bowline is a knot that makes a simple loop that is easy to tie and untie. It comes untied very easily even after a lot of strain is placed on the knot. This is a good knot for simple things such as hanging game. **I would not put my life in the hands of this knot because it comes untied so easily!**

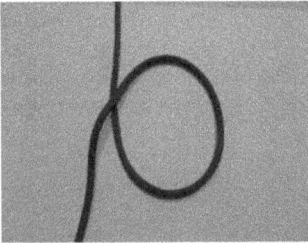

1. First form a loop around the standing end.

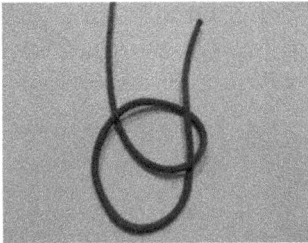

2. Bring the working end under and through the loop

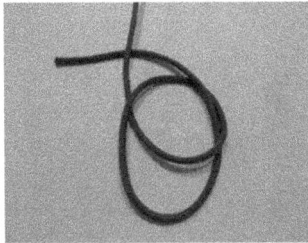

3. Take the working end behind the standing end and form another loop

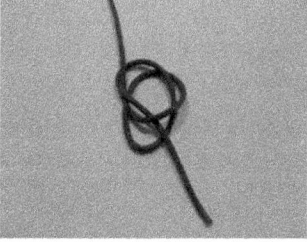

4. Finally take the working end through the first loop created and tighten

FISHERMAN'S KNOT

The fisherman's knot is a symmetrical bend made with two overhand knots tied around the standing part of the other.

A drawback of the fisherman's knot is that it can slip when tied in nylon monofilament or other slippery lines. However, if more holding strength is required you can simply double or even triple the overhand knots. It is a compact knot that jams when tightened and the working ends can be cropped very close to the knot. It is easily tied with cold, wet hands.

The steps to tying the Fisherman's Knot:

1. Lay the ropes alongside each other and tie an overhand knot in the first rope with the standing end of the other line inside the knot

2. Repeat step one with the second rope

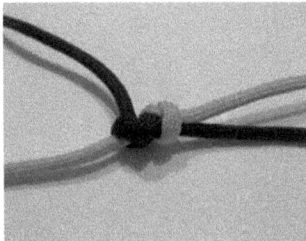

3. Tighten the two knots and pull them together

SHEET BEND

The Sheet Bend is used to join two ropes together. If the ropes are of different thickness the smaller rope should pass around the larger one. This knot can also be used to tie a rope to an eye or cargo hook for light loads. The knot is very fast to tie and is usually one of the easiest to work with.

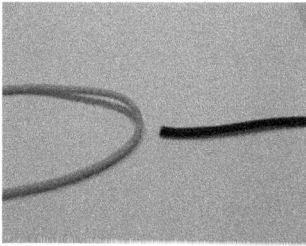

1. Form a bight (with the larger diameter rope)

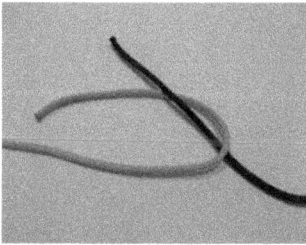

2. Insert the second rope under and then over the end of the first rope

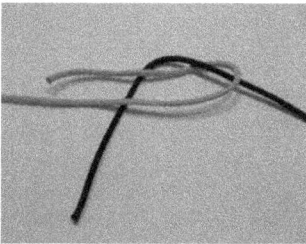

3. Take the end of the second rope and bring it under the bight

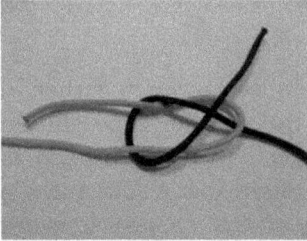

4.   Bring the end over the bight, putting it under its own standing part

5.   Pull on both standing parts to set the knot.

APPENDIX A – TIPS, TRICKS, AND HINTS

This section contains a list of tips, tricks, and shortcuts I have picked up over the course of my life and military career that make living on your own a little more tolerable and combat a little easier.

1. **Muzzle Cap** – Putting a muzzle cap on your rifle saves all kinds of hassles by reducing the amount of dust, dirt, and other garbage that could foul the barrel and cause the barrel to burst when fired or another type of weapon malfunction. You can use anything that is decently durable and will cover the muzzle but presents no real obstacle to a bullet should you have to fire the weapon. The US Military uses specially ordered muzzle caps but they are really no more than appropriately sized plastic cable guards that you should be able to purchase at any electrical supply store. If you cannot find these an unlubricated condom works very well and is what American GIs used in World War II.

2. **Bug juice & Camouflage Face Paint** – If you paint your face you will find that not only does face paint cause acne breakouts the stuff is very difficult to completely clean off. A trick is to use just about any insect repellant when you clean it off. For some reason bug juice acts a solvent that makes face paint come right off.

3. **Tent Stake Trip Wire** – US Army tent stakes have a hole in the top that is there specifically for the purpose of using the tent stake to anchor a trip wire.

4. **Treat your clothes with Permethrin** – Permethrin is an odorless, long lasting insect repellent that the military gives soldiers to treat their clothes with. It is also available commercially through a company called Insect Shield (http://www.insectshield.com/). Insect Shield sells their own clothing but you can also send your clothes to them and they will treat them for you on

per piece bass. The order form is here: <u>INSECT SHIELD YOUR OWN CLOTHES ORDER FORM</u>. We treated our clothing before deployment to Iraq and the insect repellency lasted the entire 13 month deployment and beyond.

5. **Avoid Velcro™ Pouches** – There are a bewildering variety of tactical pouches available for purchase. My one piece of advice is to avoid a pouch with a Velcro™ closure and go for straps with buckles instead. This is for the simple reason that nothing sounds louder in the woods than ripping open a Velcro pocket, especially at night.

6. **C-4 Cooking** – An old-school US Army trick to cook something quick is to use C-4 plastic explosive. A ball of C-4 the diameter of a Quarter will boil a canteen cup full of water in about 3 minutes because C-4 burns so hot. Burning it won't make it explode but do try not to stomp on it to put it out because then it **will** explode. A combination of heat & pressure will cause C-4 to detonate.

7. **Field Expedient Stove** – A common soup can makes an excellent field expedient cooking pot. Just make sure you do not take the lid off completely when opening the can so that you can bend the lid in half and use it as a handle.

8. **Condoms (unlubricated)** – These are great for waterproofing just about anything that will fit in them from a pack of cigarettes, blasting caps, to your last pack of matches.

APPENDIX B – MINEFIELD RECORD

MINEFIELD RECORD
For use of this form, see FM 3-34.210; the proponent agency is TRADOC.

DA FORM 1355, SEP 2006   DA FORM 1355, MAR 87, IS OBSOLETE.   Page 1 of 3

CARD

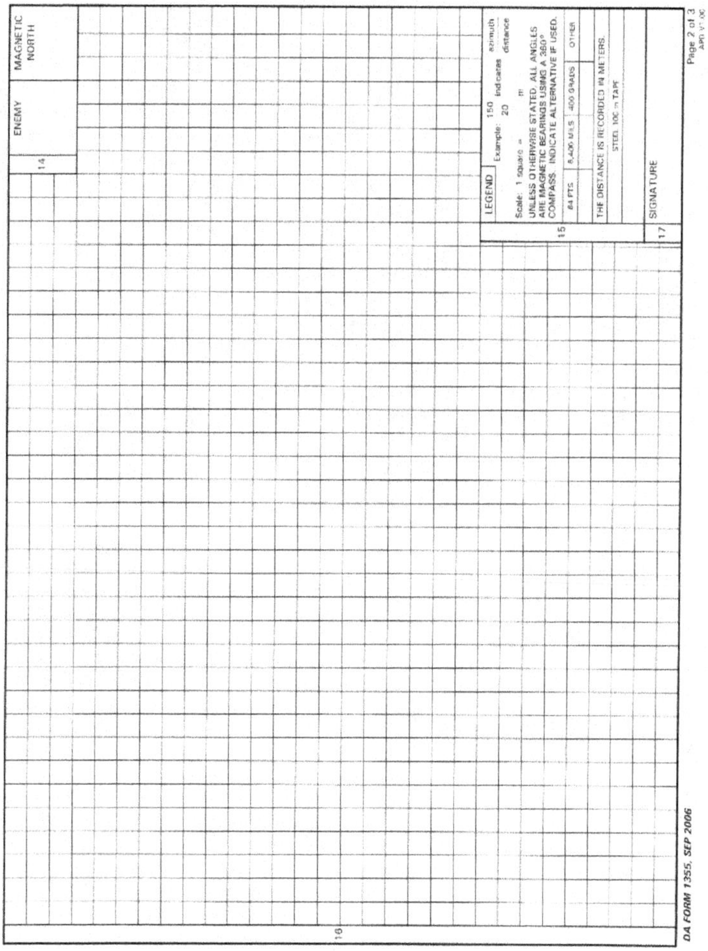

ENEMY | MAGNETIC NORTH

14

LEGEND

	azimuth	distance
	150	indicates
Example	20	m

Scale: 1 square = ____ m

UNLESS OTHERWISE STATED, ALL ANGLES ARE MAGNETIC BEARINGS USING A 360° COMPASS. INDICATE ALTERNATIVE IF USED.

| 84 FTS | 6,400 MILS | 400 GRADS | OTHER |

THE DISTANCE IS RECORDED IN METERS

STEEL 100 m TAPE

15

SIGNATURE

17

16

DA FORM 7355, SEP 2006

Page 2 of 3
APT V3C

Patrick J Shrier

INSTRUCTIONS:

The numbers correspond to numbered blocks on the form.

1. Enter complete data on the authority of laying and on the laying unit. Include the officer in charge name, rank, and SSN.

2. Enter the date-time groups for starting and completion times. Include the recorder name, rank, and SSN.

3. Enter the copy and sheet numbers. The number of copies will depend upon the unit SOP and the classification of the minefield. The number of sheets will depend upon the length and the depth of the minefield versus the scale.

4. Enter the minefield number as follows:

    Designation of unit authorizing installation

    Number of obstacle

    Status of obstacle (E - Executed, P - Proposed, U - Under Construction) —————— 3:147-lnt-2-E

5. Enter the map data as stated on the maps used.

6. Enter the complete data on at least two landmarks with 8-digit grid coordinates. Cross out unused blocks.

7. Enter descriptions of any intermediate markers used. Use an intermediate marker when a landmark is more than 200 meters from the minefield or the row reference stake cannot be seen from the landmark. Ensure that the intermediate marker is not closer than 75 meters to the row reference stake, if possible. Cross out unused blocks.

8. Describe the boundary marking.

9. Enter the number of rows laid other than the IOE. Describe the row markers (line out words that are not applicable).

10. Enter the width marking and closing provisions for each lane, when appropriate, give the type and number of mines for closing. Describe the location of these mines in the "NOTES" (Block 12). (Patrol lanes are 1 meter wide, one-way vehicular lanes are 8 meters wide, and two-way vehicular lanes are 16 meters wide.) Cross out unused blocks.

11. Enter the type of minefield by crossing out lanes that are not needed. Indicate the method of laying by marking out incorrect descriptions. Enter the types of mines as AT, APF, or APB. (Enter chemical mines under AT mines.) Enter the number of mines and antihandling devices installed in the IOE and in each row for each type of mine. Letter the rows serially, starting with the first one laid. Enter the totals. Cross out unused blocks.

12. Enter under "NOTES" information which would be useful to personnel clearing the minefield. Appropriate items include the location of chemical mines, the location of AT mines with antihandling devices, the location of AP mines with trip wires, clusters in the IOE which contain mines, where safety devices are buried, cluster composition, and numbered omitted clusters in regular strips.

13. Ensure that the officer in charge enters his signature, rank, and date.

14. Enter arrows for the direction of the enemy and the magnetic north. Ensure that the enemy arrow always points within the top 180° of the paper; the north arrow should follow one of the lines of the graph.

15. Enter the scale of the sketch for minefields; the sketch should be drawn to a scale of about 1 square = _____ meters.

16. Sketch in the following, as applicable.

  a. Show directional arrows as follows:

    (1) Landmarks (or intermediate markers) to row markers at starting and finishing points of the last row laid or to the nearest or farthest mine in a group.

    (2) From landmarks (or intermediate markers) to fence or boundary markers.

    (3) From landmarks to intermediate markers, if used.

    (4) For each straight line section of a lane centerline.

    (5) Between markers of starting points of adjacent rows, including IOE, and between finishing points of adjacent rows, including the IOE.

    (6) For each segment of the IOE, label all directional arrows with magnetic azimuth in degrees and distance in meters. Express as a fraction (for example, 247°/90 meters).

    Recorded from friendly to enemy side and from right to left or left to right.

  b. Show the approximate location of protective fences or boundary markers.

  c. Show the length and depth of the minefield in meters. (These dimensions indicate the extremities of the minefield.)

  d. Show a grid intersection and give the grid coordinates.

  e. Show a trace of shoreline and direction and approximate rate in meters per second of water current for mines laid underwater.

17. Ensure that the officer in charge enters his signature and rank when complete.

DA FORM 1355, SEP 2006

APPENDIX C – FOODBORNE ILLNESSES

ILLNESS NAME	FOOD INVOLVED	ONSET	SYMPTOMS	PREVENTION
Bacillus cereus (Food Poisoning)	Grains, including rice, flour, dry-mix products.	1-16 hours	Diarrhea, abdominal pain, nausea, and vomiting	Do not hold prepared foods at room temperature. Keep dry foods and mixes dry.
Botulism (Food Poisoning)	Inadequately processed, usually home canned, low acid foods, meat and fish.	12-36 hours	Difficulty in swallowing, weakness, dizziness, voice changes.	Toxin destroyed by boiling. Cook foods thoroughly.

Clostridium perfrinigens (Food Poisoning)	Stews, meat pies or meat gravies held at warm temperatures.	6-24 hours	Nausea, sometimes vomiting, colicky pains, diarrhea	Thoroughly cook foods. Hold at 150°F or more.
Staphylococcus aureus (Food Poisoning)	Cooked ham, salads of protein food, custard pastries, Hollandaise sauce, warmed over food.	1-6 hours	Nausea, vomiting, diarrhea, acute prostration, abdominal cramps.	Thoroughly cook foods. Hold at 150°F or more. Keep hands clean and skin sore-free.
Campylobacter (Diarrhea)	Raw milk, uncooked chicken, raw hamburger, water.	1-10 days	Nausea, cramps, headache, sometimes fever, diarrhea.	Cook foods thoroughly. Use boiled or treated water.
E. coli 0 157:H7 (Diarrhea)	Ground beef, water.	12-72 hours	Abdominal cramps, bloody diarrhea, fever, vomiting.	Cook foods thoroughly. Use boiled or treated water. Clean Hands

Shigella (dysentery)	Moist foods, salads, dairy products, contaminated water.	1-7 days	Diarrhea, fever, vomiting, cramps.	Thorough cooking. Strict cleanliness when handling food.
Listeriosis	Milk products, unwashed vegetables, raw or improperly processed wild and domestic meats.	4 days to 3 weeks	Flu-like symptoms with fever and nausea. Pregnancy interruption.	Cook meats thoroughly. Use only pasteurized dairy products. Avoid eating unwashed vegetables or raw meats.
Salmonellosis	Inadequately cooked poultry, eggs or food containing them. Meat or dairy products.	6-72 hours	Abdominal pain, diarrhea, chills, fever, frequent vomiting, prostration.	Cook foods thoroughly. Use boiled or treated water. Clean Hands Sanitized Utensils and surfaces.

Hepatitis A	Raw seafood from polluted waters, food contaminated by infected handler, polluted water.	15-50 days	Nausea, abdominal pain, weakness and discomfort, fever.	Cook meats thoroughly. Use only pasteurized dairy products. Avoid eating unwashed vegetables or raw meats. Use boiled or treated water.
Vincent's angina (Trench Mouth)	Unsanitized utensils, glasses, containers.	3-5 days	Soar throat, bleeding gums, pain.	Sanitization of equipment. Good oral hygiene.
Norwalk virus (viral gastroenteritis)	Beef, chicken, pork or pork products, Meat salads, vegetable salads, salad dressings.	10-51 hours	Diarrhea, abdominal cramps, nausea, vomiting, fever.	Thoroughly cook foods. Hold at 150°F or more.

Tapeworm	Insufficiently cooked beef, pork or fish products.	3-6 weeks	Nervousness, insomnia, loss of weight, abdominal pain, nausea, diarrhea, anemia.	Cook meat and fish thoroughly. Inspect carefully.
Trichinosis	Raw or insufficiently cooked pork or pork products, and pork products mixed in beef.	1-45 days	Swollen eyelids, diarrhea, muscle soreness, thirst, sweating, chills, weakness, intermittent high fever.	Cook pork and pork products thoroughly to a temperature of 165°F or more.

Source – US Centers for Disease Control and Prevention.

REFERENCE LIST

This is a list of books and other resources that, in addition to this one, will come in handy in any type of survival situation. One thing to keep in mind as you peruse survivalist or prepper websites is that there are literally hundreds of them out there and many trend towards surrealism in their ideas. I am talking here about the many claims that vaccines cause autism, chemtrails, fluoride in the water as mind control, fracking causing earthquakes, and other equally zany ideas. My advice is to look at all these sites with a grain of salt when it comes to them talking anything political and perform your own critical analysis of such claims. If you believe them then great, that is up to you. If you don't believe them that is great too. Regardless, many of these sites have some excellent tip and ideas on what to do, buy, train, and otherwise prepare for bad things to happen.

1. US Army Field & Training Manuals: All of these can be purchased through major booksellers. If they are available online I have included the link for free copies below. Of course, online copies must be printed as the internet will no longer be available in a survival situation.
   a. FM 3-25.26 Map Reading and Land Navigation University of Vermont
   b. FM 3-90-1 Offense and Defense Volume 1: Globalsecurity.org (Limited number of free downloads)
   c. FM 4-25-1 First Aid: Globalsecurity.org
   d. FM 4-25.12 Unit Field Hygiene Team: Globalsecurity.org
   e. FM 5-15 Field Fortifications
   f. FM 5-19 Composite Risk Management: US US Army

g. FM 5-33 Terrain Analysis: <u>BITS</u>

h. FM 5-103 Survivability: <u>Armageddon Online</u>

i. FM 17-98 The Cavalry Scout Platoon

j. FM 20-3 Camouflage, Concealment, and Decoys: <u>Scribd</u> (must purchase to download)

k. FM 21-75 The Warrior Ethos and

l. Soldier Combat Skills: <u>Globalsecurity.org</u>

m. FM 21-76 Survival: <u>Globalsecurity.org</u>

n. FM 90-7 Combined Arms Obstacle Integration: <u>Military Field Manuals.net</u>

o. SH 21-76 Ranger Handbook: <u>US Army Ranger School</u>

p. TM 31-210 <u>Improvised Munitions Handbook</u>

2. Other Printed Works

a. The 12 Foxfire books: Available for purchase on Amazon or directly from the <u>Foxfire Museum Gift shop</u>

b. The Ranger Handbook

3. Online Resources

a. <u>Armageddon</u> <u>Online</u> (<u>http://www.armageddononline.org</u>): A good site that has both a forum, articles, and a huge database of downloadable books

b. <u>The</u> <u>Survival</u> <u>Blog</u> (<u>http://www.survivalblog.com</u>): James Wesley Rawles' site where he hosts a lot of information on the topics of survival and disaster preparedness.

c. <u>Military</u> <u>Field</u> <u>Manuals</u> (<u>http://www.militaryfieldmanuals.net/</u>): A great site that has a large collection of military FM's available for free download.

d. <u>netknots.com</u> (<u>http://www.netknots.com/</u>: An excellent resource for how to tie knots

e. <u>The</u> <u>Survivalist</u> <u>Blog</u> (<u>http://www.thesurvivalistblog.net/</u>): A great site full of realistic thinking and appraisals of what is necessary in a survival situation

f. <u>Backdoor</u> <u>Survival</u> (<u>http://www.backdoorsurvival.com/</u>): This site has quite a bit of good First Aid advice as well as more information on food storage

g. Primitive Ways (http://www.primitiveways.com/index.html) Interesting website that has instructions for constructing many pre-industrial items from bows to baskets

h. The Survival Doctor (http://www.thesurvivaldoctor.com/): Lots of useful First Aid and medical advice for when a doctor is far away or otherwise unavailable.

i. The Ready Store (http://www.thereadystore.com/blog/) Tons of useful tips for everything from how to hunt to how to farm for yourself. The also sell stuff.

j. Willow Haven Outdoor (http://willowhavenoutdoor.com/) Willow Haven offers plenty of advice on their page but is also an example of the kinds of company that offer hands-on training classes in survival skills.

k. Sirvivaltek.com (http://survivaltek.com/) Another site that has plenty of information but which also offers hands on training.

These are just a starting point and some of the most useful sites I have found. When you get ready to start buying things and building your own bags and kits shop around, both locally and on the internet. One of my personal favorite shopping sites is Amazon, they have just about everything and often they have the lowest prices

GLOSSARY

- Angular Mil: A unit of angular measure. In NATO usage there are 6400 mils in a full circle, used to calculate precise azimuths in land navigation. Most commonly referred to as simply mil

- Avenue of Approach: The area from which an opponent is traveling. Also can be terrain features that are suitable for the movement of yourself or an opponent

- Bend: A knot for joining two knots together

- Bight: Generally this means an arc in the rope that makes a semicircle; it can also mean just the part in between the standing and working ends of the rope.

- Bough Shelter: Improvised shelter constructed from a fallen pine tree

- Bug-Out-Bag (B.O.B.): A bag that contains the minimum necessary equipment to survive for an indeterminate length of time. It is pre-packed and available with minimal (2-4 hours) notice should it be necessary to evacuate an area.

- Contact: Actually trading fire or in combat with an armed opponent

- Course of Action (COA): Any sequence of activities that an individual or group may follow to accomplish a stated objective

- Deadfall: Trees that have died and fallen naturally in the forest or the piles of leftover unusable branches tossed aside after logging an area is complete. Deadfall is an excellent source of dry wood for fires and construction of shelters

- Degree: A unit of angular measure in which there are 360 arc degrees in a full circle, used to calculate azimuths in land navigation. Most commonly referred to as simply degree.

- Flank: The sides of an opponent's avenue of approach. Distinct from the front or rear

- Food Poisoning: Any of a number of foodborne pathogens that cause illness which general manifests as nausea, headache, diarrhea, and vomiting. Can be life threatening if untreated

- Go-To-Hell-Kit (G.O.T.H.): A kit that that contains the minimum necessary equipment to survive for a minimum of 72-96 hours. It is pre-packed and available at a moment's notice should it be necessary to evacuate an area until the B.O.B. Bag can be retrieved

- Hitch: A knot used to attach a rope to an object such as a ring, post, or another rope

- Lashing: A knot used to tie two or more objects together rigidly

- Lean-to: Improvised shelter constructed with a length of cord and tarp or poncho

- Loop: A section of the bight that makes a circle and crosses over itself

- Meter: 100 centimeters. The standard length of measure using the metric system. Approximately 39 American Inches. The meter is often used interchangeably with the Yard but this s to be avoided as at any useful distance the difference between the two measures is quite large

- Map: A graphic representation of a portion of the earth's surface drawn to scale, as seen from above

- Military Crest: The highest spot on a hill below the natural crest where a person can stand and not be silhouetted against the skyline to an observer at the base of the slope

- Military Decision Making Process (MDMP): A formalized step-by-step guide to analyzing a situation and determining the best Course of Action

- Murphy's Law: A truism in military operations that holds that *"anything that can go wrong, will; and probably at the worst possible time."*

- Objective: Stated goal of an individual or party. This can be either a task or a location

- Obstacle: Any feature, natural or manmade, that works to obstruct the free movement of a force, friendly or enemy

- Rear: The side of an enemy avenue of approach away from friendly elements in contact

- Scale: A proportion used in determining the dimensional relationship of a representation to that which it represents

- Sinnet: A braid used to store ropes by shortening the overall length of the rope or cord

- Standing End: The standing end of a rope is the part not active in knot tying (i.e. just lying there passively)

- Topographic Map: Map that graphically represents the terrain features to be found in defined area.

- Whipping: A binding tied around the end of a rope to keep it from unraveling

- Working End: The working end of a rope is the part that is active in knot tying (i.e. the end of the rope manipulated)

- Yard: 36 American inches or 3 Feet.